Pirates

History

The History of the Pirates That Plagued the New World

(The True and Surprising Story of the Pirates of the Caribbean)

John McClellan

Published By **George Denver**

John McClellan

All Rights Reserved

Pirates History: The History of the Pirates That Plagued the New World (The True and Surprising Story of the Pirates of the Caribbean)

ISBN 978-0-9952939-6-0

No part of this guidebook shall be reproduced in any form without permission in writing from the publisher except in the case of brief quotations embodied in critical articles or reviews.

Legal & Disclaimer

The information contained in this book is not designed to replace or take the place of any form of medicine or professional medical advice. The information in this book has been provided for educational & entertainment purposes only.

The information contained in this book has been compiled from sources deemed reliable, and it is accurate to the best of the Author's knowledge; however, the Author cannot guarantee its accuracy and validity and cannot be held liable for any errors or omissions. Changes are periodically made to this book. You must consult your doctor or get professional medical advice before using any of the suggested remedies, techniques, or information in this book.

Upon using the information contained in this book, you agree to hold harmless the Author from and against any damages, costs, and expenses, including any legal fees potentially resulting from the application of any of the information provided by this guide. This disclaimer applies to any damages or injury caused by the use and application, whether directly or indirectly, of any advice or information presented, whether for breach of contract, tort, negligence, personal injury, criminal intent, or under any other cause of action.

You agree to accept all risks of using the information presented inside this book. You need to consult a professional medical practitioner in order to ensure you are both able and healthy enough to participate in this program.

Table Of Contents

Chapter 1: The Dawn Of Piracy 1

Chapter 2: The Golden Age Of Pirates Begins 11

Chapter 3: Defying Conventions 21

Chapter 4: The Pirate Round 38

Chapter 5: The Notorious Captain Kidd .. 52

Chapter 6: The Pirate Republic Of Nassau 67

Chapter 7: Famous Naval Battles Against Pirates 81

Chapter 8: Blackbeard 88

Chapter 9: Captain Kidd 103

Chapter 10: Stede Bonnet 117

Chapter 11: Charles Vane 131

Chapter 12: William Fly 146

Chapter 13: Bartolomeu Português 163

Chapter 14: Thomas White 177

Chapter 1: The Dawn Of Piracy

In the annals of maritime information, a shadowy and fascinating generation emerges due to the fact the sunrise of piracy. Stretching back to antiquity, the roots of piracy may be traced through the while, revealing a complex tapestry woven with intrigue, desperation, and a thirst for adventure upon the large expanse of the world's oceans.

To delve into the origins of piracy, one should peer into the mists of time, in which the earliest times of sea raiding echo through legends and historic payments. In the Mediterranean, the notorious Cilician pirates carved a fearsome reputation in the first millennium BCE, preying upon trade routes and placing terror into the hearts of investors and sailors alike. Their audacity and foxy laid a foundation for what ought to become a undying tale of renegades and rogues.

Moving in advance in records, the Phoenicians, those intrepid seafarers, engaged in a form of prepared piracy as they prolonged there have an effect on in some unspecified time in the future of the ancient global. Their mastery of maritime exchange intertwined with opportunistic acts of piracy, showcasing the early symbiotic dating amongst legitimate trade and illicit plunder.

As civilizations burgeoned and crumbled, the decline of the Roman Empire ushered in an technology of turmoil that supplied fertile floor for piracy's emergence. The crumble of centralized authority within the Western Mediterranean left seafaring routes liable to marauders. The Vandalic and Gothic invasions, coupled with the autumn of Carthage, similarly destabilized the maritime landscape, predominant to a surge in pirate interest.

It have become the maritime powerhouses of the Middle Ages – the Vikings and Norse raiders – who pushed the limits of piracy.

Driven with the resource of expansionist dreams and a look for riches, the ones fierce warriors plundered coastal settlements, forging a legacy of piracy that left a profound effect at the collective imagination. The Viking Age, marked thru formidable longship raids and brutal raids on unsuspecting businesses, fashioned the perception of pirates as seafaring brigands.

The evolution of piracy took a dramatic flip all through the Age of Exploration. As European powers released into voyages of discovery, newly mounted change routes traversing the Atlantic and Pacific Oceans beckoned bold adventurers to make the maximum the uncertainties of the open seas. Privateering, a rustic-sanctioned shape of piracy, grow to be born. Governments issued "letters of marque," efficaciously granting licenses for personal ships to seize enemy vessels. The lines amongst piracy and valid war blurred as privateers straddled legality, amassing wealth thru plunder below the guise of serving their countries.

However, the ones early manifestations of piracy have been no longer truely driven thru lawlessness and greed. For many, piracy modified right right into a reaction to financial inequalities, oppressive rule, and the lack of opportunity opportunities. This underlying socio-economic context lent piracy an element of complexity, highlighting the regularly nuanced motivations that propelled males and females to take to the excessive seas.

Intriguingly, the phenomenon of piracy grow to be not restricted to the West. The South China Sea witnessed the upward push of pirates who capitalized at the difficult waterways and bustling alternate routes of East Asia. These pirates, known as wokou in China and wako in Japan, seized possibilities all through durations of political turmoil and social unrest.

As the winds of data carried civilization in advance, piracy's dawn forged an prolonged shadow, leaving an indelible mark on humanity's adventure through time. The origins of piracy, woven from strands of ambition, desperation, and defiance, offer a compelling narrative that sets the extent for the turbulent and captivating chapters that might spread at the excessive seas.

Ancient Seafaring Raiders

In the expansive tapestry of information, the pages are decorated with tales of historical seafaring raiders whose exploits have etched their names into the annals of time. Long before the time period "pirate" emerged, those bold mariners navigated the tumultuous waters of antiquity, shaping the course of maritime narratives with their audacious raids and formidable seafaring prowess.

Among the earliest examples of ancient seafaring raiders are the Sea Peoples, an enigmatic confederation of maritime raiders who surged onto the historical degree within the direction of the Bronze Age fall apart around 1200 BCE. These marauders, hailing from numerous areas for the duration of the Mediterranean, orchestrated waves of attacks on coastal settlements, leaving in the back of a direction of destruction and upheaval. While their origins remain shrouded in mystery, their effect at the ancient international became easy, as their invasions contributed to the autumn of severa effective civilizations of the time.

The Greek and Roman worlds also bore witness to the upward thrust of seafaring raiders who navigated the Mediterranean with every ambition and ferocity. The Illyrians, population of the western Balkans, carved a reputation as bold maritime raiders, plundering coastal cities and installing fortified bases to release their attacks. Their nimble ships and seafaring prowess allowed them to strike rapidly and prevent pursuit, earning them both fear and grudging recognize from their contemporaries.

In the East, the Phoenicians, renowned as hold close sailors and consumers, were no longer exempt from assignment seafaring raiding. While their maritime empire in huge detail revolved round legitimate change and colonization, they were seemed to have interaction in opportunistic raids to steady assets or expand their effect. This twin nature of the Phoenicians as every investors and capacity raiders underscored the complicated interplay amongst financial pursuits and acts of maritime aggression.

Venturing farther east, the Indian Ocean bore witness to the Austronesian growth and the seafaring prowess of historical Polynesian and Micronesian cultures. These intrepid navigators launched into voyages of exploration and migration, traversing massive stretches of open water with superb navigational talents and complex boat-constructing strategies. Their voyages intertwined exchange, exploration, and settlement, laying the inspiration for the interconnected maritime global of the Indian Ocean.

The legacy of historic seafaring raiders extended beyond the Mediterranean and Indian Ocean. The Germanic tribes that inhabited the North Sea and the Baltic Sea, along with the Saxons and Vikings, left an indelible mark on history. The Vikings, specially, became synonymous with seafaring raids, using their iconic longships to plunder and overcome a ways off lands. Their expeditions, beginning from coastal raids to complete-fledged invasions of England, France, and past, reshaped the political and cultural panorama of medieval Europe.

As the ebb and go together with the waft of information carried these historic seafaring raiders all through large oceans and via tumultuous eras, their legacy stays printed on the fabric of civilization. From the enigmatic Sea Peoples to the audacious Vikings, those mariners navigated uncharted waters, leaving a direction of legends, artifacts, and archaeological proof that preserve to captivate modern-day-day-day imaginations. The exploits of those early raiders provide a window into the dynamic interplay amongst human ambition, maritime exploration, and the ever-changing currents of records.

Pirates of the Mediterranean

Within the solar-soaking wet expanse of the Mediterranean Sea, a wealthy tapestry of seafaring information is interwoven with the testimonies of pirates who as quickly as roamed its azure waters. From the ancient global to the medieval a while, the Mediterranean bore witness to the upward push and fall of pirates who left an indelible mark at the course of maritime narratives, shaping the destinies of empires and civilizations.

The maritime information of the Mediterranean dates decrease again millennia, with seafaring cultures just like the Phoenicians and Greeks putting in bustling exchange routes that crisscrossed the sea's significant expanse. However, along legitimate change, piracy emerged as a chronic mission. In the ancient global, piracy grow to be often an opportunistic mission, pushed through the appeal of capturing valuable cargo and the strategic gain of controlling key maritime passages.

During the tumultuous instances following the fall apart of the Western Roman Empire, the Mediterranean have become a breeding floor for piracy. As political instability and economic decline gripped the region, coastal settlements determined themselves prone to marauders who took benefit of the chaos. The Vandals, a Germanic tribe that set up a state in North Africa, used their naval prowess to launch devastating raids on coastal cities and islands, disrupting exchange and sowing fear at some degree inside the area.

Chapter 2: The Golden Age Of Pirates Begins

In the annals of maritime information, a financial disaster of exceptional audacity and intrigue unfolds with the sunrise of the Golden Age of Pirates. This generation, spanning greater or much less from the overdue 17th century to the early 18th century, observed the upward push of mythical figures and crews who carved their names into the lore of the excessive seas, all the time changing the belief of piracy and leaving an indelible mark on well-known manner of existence.

The decline of traditional naval powers and the unchecked boom of transatlantic alternate routes set the extent for the emergence of piracy as a thriving business enterprise. Following the Treaty of Utrecht in 1713, which ended the War of the Spanish Succession, heaps of sailors located themselves unemployed and adrift in a worldwide though grappling with geopolitical instability. Many became to piracy as a method of survival and revenge in opposition to a system they considered as unjust.

One of the maximum iconic pirates of this period emerge as the infamous Blackbeard, whose actual name changed into in all likelihood Edward Teach. Operating within the West Indies and along the American coast, Blackbeard's fearsome look – embellished with lit fuses twisted into his beard – struck terror into the hearts of folks who crossed his path. His ship, the Queen Anne's Revenge, have turn out to be a photo of piracy's energy and audacity.

The Caribbean, with its complex community of islands and sea routes, have turn out to be a haven for pirates searching for each riches and secure haven. The pirate republic of Nassau within the Bahamas stands as a testament to the lawless but democratic society that emerged, in which pirates lived by way of way in their non-public code and elected their leaders. Port Royal, as soon as a British stronghold, transformed right into a pirate haven, fostering an environment in which marauders ought to discover camaraderie and percentage within the spoils of their plunder.

Anne Bonny and Mary Read, two ladies who defied the norms of their time, joined the ranks of pirates throughout this period. Dressed as men, they participated in piracy alongside their male opposite numbers, demonstrating that the attraction of adventure and wealth modified into now not constrained to gender boundaries. Their recollections keep to encourage reminiscences of robust and unbiased ladies in records.

The immoderate seas inside the path of the Golden Age have been a theatre of daring and audacity, as pirates commandeered rapid and nimble vessels known as sloops and schooners. Their processes often worried surprise attacks, intimidation, and the effective use of cannons to overpower carrier enterprise ships and naval vessels alike. The

Jolly Roger, the iconic skull-and-crossbones flag, struck worry into sufferers and signaled the presence of pirates at the horizon.

The notorious pirate code, popularized through manner of fictional debts but rooted in ancient truths, stated a set of guidelines that governed the conduct and department of spoils amongst pirate crews. This code sought to preserve order, cohesion, and fairness amongst a severa and regularly ragtag institution of people united thru the use of a commonplace cause – the pursuit of wealth and adventure.

The decline of the Golden Age come to be added approximately via numerous elements. Increasing naval pressure, combined with efforts to suppress piracy and shield provider provider hobbies, eroded the pirates' dominion over the seas. The hanging of infamous pirates which includes Blackbeard and the seize of pirate strongholds signaled the start of the forestall for this period. The maritime international slowly transitioned into a state-of-the-art era of maritime regulation and manage.

The Golden Age of Pirates, a time of romanticized lawlessness and ambitious escapades, left an indelible mark on maritime records and famous manner of existence. The exploits of figures like Blackbeard, Anne Bonny, and the pirate havens of the Caribbean hold to captivate imaginations, inspiring memories of journey, rebel, and the attraction of existence at the open sea. This economic smash in information showcases the complicated interaction amongst societal upheaval, financial opportunity, and the timeless appeal of the pirate's life.

Buccaneers of the Caribbean

In the sun-soaked waters of the Caribbean Sea, a swashbuckling tale of adventure, riches, and bold escapades unfurls with the rise of the buccaneers. These rugged privateers, often taking walks on the fringes of legality, left an indelible mark at the maritime history of the New World all through the seventeenth century. Born out of a completely particular confluence of occasions, the buccaneers navigated the treacherous waters of politics, commerce, and battle with a mixture of audacity and cunning that defined an era.

The time period "buccaneer" itself traces its origins to the Caribbean's wild and untamed panorama. These mariners, regularly escaping lives of trouble and oppression, sought safe haven on the islands and beaches of the place. Hunting wild farm animals referred to as "boucan," they smoked the beef over open fires, growing a portable food supply that sustained them for the duration of their maritime endeavors. This exercise, mixed with their seafaring abilties, set the degree for the buccaneers' emergence as maritime predators.

Amidst the unstable backdrop of European colonial rivalries, the buccaneers exploited the electricity struggles amongst countries to installation a foothold inside the Caribbean.

While a few had been legitimate privateers, preserving letters of marque from European powers that jail them to attack enemy vessels, others straddled the road between privateer and pirate, switching allegiances and goals as opportunities arose. This dual nature allowed buccaneers to perform in a criminal grey place, leveraging the complexity of worldwide contributors of the own family to their advantage.

One of the maximum well-known buccaneers of the era became Sir Henry Morgan. Appointed as a privateer through the usage of the English Crown, Morgan led formidable raids on Spanish-held territories, taking pics cities, plundering riches, and placing fear into the hearts of his enemies. His audacious sack of Panama in 1671, a feat that shook the policies of the Spanish Empire, cemented his recognition as a legendary figure in buccaneer lore.

The buccaneers' operational techniques had been characterized thru their intimate facts of the Caribbean's geography, allowing them to make the most hidden coves, shallow waters, and uncharted passages to their gain. Their quick vessels, regularly smaller and more maneuverable than traditional naval ships, allowed them to navigate those treacherous waters with relative ease, escaping pursuit and launching surprise attacks.

The buccaneers' exploits had been no longer constrained to maritime raids by myself. They installed fortified bases on a protracted way flung islands, growing havens wherein they'll restore and refit their vessels, divide their plunder, and plan their next ventures. The island of Tortuga, placed off the coast of Hispaniola, emerged as a notorious pirate stronghold and a melting pot of numerous nationalities, united thru their shared aspirations for wealth and adventure.

However, the buccaneers' golden age have become no longer destined to last. The Treaty of Madrid in 1670 and the following Treaty of Ryswick in 1697 aimed to curtail the buccaneers' activities via the usage of setting up new borders and territorial obstacles some of the colonial powers. With the emergence of extra today's naval forces and the tightening grip of imperial manage, the buccaneers' days as freebooters came to an surrender.

The buccaneers of the Caribbean, with their ambitious exploits and colourful personalities, stand as a testomony to the intersection of possibility, ambition, and the complicated geopolitical dynamics of the New World. Their legacy keeps to captivate the creativeness, embodying the attraction of lifestyles at the excessive seas and the indomitable spirit of people who sought to navigate a path to riches, freedom, and journey amidst the turbulent waters of the Caribbean.

The Infamous Blackbeard

Within the annals of pirate information, few names evoke the equal feel of fear and awe as that of the infamous Blackbeard. Born as Edward Teach, possibly in Bristol, England, at some degree inside the early 1680s, he would pass at once to come to be one of the most iconic and enigmatic figures of the Golden Age of Piracy. Blackbeard's legacy, shrouded in a mixture of reality and legend, remains etched inside the maritime memories of ambitious escapades and audacious exploits.

Blackbeard's transformation from a younger seaman to a feared pirate started out out as he joined the group of the privateer deliver Queen Anne's Revenge, commanded by means of way of using the pirate Benjamin Hornigold. This alliance may feature a turning factor in Blackbeard's life, propelling him proper right into a world of lawlessness and maritime plunder. As Hornigold's protege, Blackbeard observed the strategies and strategies that might later outline his very very very own piratical career.

Chapter 3: Defying Conventions

In the annals of maritime facts, the recollections of ladies pirates stand as inspiring testament to the indomitable spirit of people who dared to defy societal norms and navigate the treacherous waters of the immoderate seas. These remarkable girls, frequently relegated to the margins of records, carved their very own paths in an generation dominated thru guys, difficult conventions and leaving an indelible mark on the world of piracy.

The pirate global, traditionally ruled with the aid of the usage of manner of male crews, have end up no longer impervious to the have an effect on of women. While woman pirates have been a minority, their presence became felt from the early days of piracy to the Golden Age and beyond. Anne Bonny and Mary Read, two of the maximum renowned girl pirates, emerged sooner or later of the Golden Age of Piracy and their recollections function a compelling window into the lives of ladies who dared to take to the open sea.

Anne Bonny, born in Ireland in the overdue seventeenth century, sailed the Caribbean alongside her lover, Calico Jack Rackham. Disguised as a person, Anne become a effective fighter who commanded admire among her male crewmates. Her boldness and tenacity have been on complete show at the same time as the institution changed into captured, with Anne defiantly putting forward that she "pleaded her belly" to eliminate her execution due to her being pregnant. Though her final future stays unsure, Anne's legacy as a fierce woman pirate endures.

Mary Read, a few other parent who defied gender conventions, moreover determined herself entangled in piracy. Raised as a boy thru her mother, Mary joined the British military and later a pirate enterprise beneath the command of Calico Jack. Like Anne Bonny, Mary's talent in fight and backbone to thrive in a male-dominated international made her a remarkable presence on the ship. Her proper identification come to be positioned after capture, and her destiny intertwined with

Anne's inside the route in their trial and imprisonment.

But the recollections of ladies pirates do not surrender with Anne Bonny and Mary Read. Women pirates were determined in numerous cultures and eras. In China, for instance, the 19th-century pirate Ching Shih commanded a fleet of loads of ships and masses of pirates, terrorizing the South China Sea. Her strict code of behavior and brilliant management skills solidified her popularity as one in every of records's maximum bold pirates.

The motivations at the back of girls's participation in piracy varied. For some, it changed right into a quest for independence and journey, on the equal time as for others, piracy supplied a means of survival in a worldwide that often denied women commercial enterprise employer and economic opportunities. The pirate existence allowed them to break out societal expectancies and assert themselves on an equal footing with men, as a minimum within the confines of the pirate organization.

The legacy of ladies pirates prolonged beyond their person recollections. Their defiance of gender norms and their contributions to piracy paved the manner for narratives that celebrated strong and independent girls, difficult preconceptions about girls's roles in data. The memories of Anne Bonny, Mary Read, Ching Shih, and others feature a testament to the power of human resilience and the enduring effect of individuals who dared to forge their very personal destinies amidst the tumultuous tides of the pirate worldwide.

Pirate Havens and Hideouts

In the difficult tapestry of pirate data, the idea of havens and hideouts holds a pivotal function, offering a fascinating glimpse into the clandestine worldwide of maritime brigands. Pirates, often hunted with the useful resource of naval government and competing privateers, sought stable haven in a long way flung and strategically positioned locations in which they could restore their vessels, divide their spoils, and avoid the clutches of justice. These sanctuaries, hidden the numerous uncharted nooks of the arena's coastlines and islands, performed a important function in maintaining the maritime outlaws in their time.

The appeal of pirate havens lay of their secluded nature, making them the right locations for pirates to escape the watchful eyes of the law. These hideouts ranged from remoted coves and inlets to complete islands that have been no longer best difficult for government to discover but additionally supplied critical resources for the pirates' survival. The Caribbean, with its labyrinthine waterways and abundance of a long way off islands, come to be mainly fertile floor for the recognition quo of pirate hideouts.

One of the most infamous pirate havens changed into Nassau within the Bahamas. Once a lawless outpost appeared for its brief populace of criminals, Nassau converted right right into a thriving pirate republic in some unspecified time in the future of the Golden Age of Piracy. Pirates from all corners of the Caribbean converged on this shelter, wherein they will pick out their leaders, installation their very very very own codes of conduct, and percent inside the riches received through plunder. The pirate republic of Nassau embodied the spirit of defiance and autonomy that defined the pirate global.

Tortuga, an island located off the coast of Hispaniola, changed into another renowned pirate haven at some point of the seventeenth century. This strategically positioned island supplied pirates with a base from which they'll release raids on Spanish and French ships passing through the Caribbean. Tortuga's wild terrain and hidden coves made it a notable sanctuary for pirates seeking out to interrupt out the draw close of their pursuers.

The island of Madagascar, located off the east coast of Africa, have come to be a haven for pirates called the "Brethren of the Coast." This numerous commercial enterprise employer of pirates, hailing from various elements of the area, set up a lawless society on the island's seashores. In an surroundings in which survival become paramount, the pirates banded together, forming a crude but powerful governing shape that allowed them to thrive regardless of their outlaw recognition.

Pirate havens were now not absolutely restrained to the Caribbean and Madagascar. The Indian Ocean, with its hard community of change routes, additionally hosted pirate hideouts. The island of Sainte-Marie, off the coast of Madagascar, come to be called a steady haven for pirates who sought safe haven after raiding East India Company vessels. These pirates set up agencies where they may spend their unwell-gotten earnings and break out the clutches of naval authorities.

The dynamic interaction amongst pirate havens and the broader pirate global showcased the ingenuity and resourcefulness of these maritime outlaws. These sanctuaries had been now not in reality physical locations however moreover symbolic representations of the pirates' defiance in competition to the dominant powers in their time. Pirate havens stood as a testament to the pirates' ability to carve out their very personal areas in a global that frequently sought to suppress and eliminate their manner of existence.

The Code of the Brethren

In the annals of pirate lore, the "Code of the Brethren" emerges as a fascinating and complex aspect of pirate culture throughout the Golden Age of Piracy. This unwritten however extensively diagnosed set of policies and hints ruled the behavior of pirates, supplying a unique belief into the internal workings of the pirate global. The Code of the Brethren, born out of necessity and a shared information of the stressful conditions pirates confronted, underscored the pirates' enjoy of camaraderie and their tries to set up order inner a chaotic existence.

While the perception of a regular pirate code may also evoke snap shots of a strict, dogmatic set of recommendations, the fact end up far greater nuanced. The Code of the Brethren modified into characterised with the aid of a combination of practical hints, ethical principles, and a bendy approach that allowed for adaptability inside the ever-converting worldwide of piracy. Pirates, often going for walks in free and transferring alliances, desired a framework that could stability their person hobbies with the collective suitable in their group.

One of the vital tenets of the pirate code became the principle of equality. Pirates, drawn from numerous backgrounds and cultures, have been united by a not unusual pursuit of wealth and adventure. Regardless in their origins, pirates had been equal individuals in their organization, with choices and spoils distributed pretty among all. This egalitarian method become in stark evaluation to the hierarchical structures of the naval and provider agency vessels they frequently centered.

The branch of plunder became a vital element of the pirate code. Pirates believed that a truthful distribution of wealth changed into essential to maintaining team morale and harmony. This frequently worried the quartermaster, an elected function inside the group, overseeing the branch of spoils, making sure that each member acquired an equitable percent. The quartermaster moreover executed a feature in resolving disputes and implementing the code's provisions.

Another component of the code revolved spherical issues of governance and choice-making. Captains were elected via the organization and held authority handiest inside the direction of a ship's voyage. These captains had been held answerable for their selections, and the organization need to vote to update them in the event that they felt their pastimes have been now not being efficaciously represented. This democratic method allowed pirates to have a say in the direction of their endeavors and keep a experience of organization.

The code additionally addressed issues of area and conduct. Acts of insubordination, robbery, or violence in the path of fellow company members had been strictly prohibited. Quarrels and disputes have been frequently settled via mediation, and the offending birthday celebration could probably face punishment beginning from fines to marooning on a deserted island. This emphasis on preserving order inside the organization changed into crucial to save you inner strife that would jeopardize the success of a pirate task.

While the Code of the Brethren changed into not a right written report, it turn out to be upheld thru oral lifestyle, unwavering adherence to fantastic thoughts, and the shared know-how among pirates. Its lifestyles pondered the pirates' tries to establish a sense of justice and order inner an inherently lawless and chaotic environment. The code's legacy endures in well-known way of lifestyles, immortalizing the notion of the pirate's honor, equity, and understand for their fellow crewmates. The Code of the Brethren offers a charming glimpse into the complex international of pirates, in which pragmatic worries blended with beliefs of brotherly love and equality to create a totally precise and enduring set of thoughts.

Privateers and State-Sanctioned Piracy

Amidst the tumultuous currents of maritime data, the complicated interplay among privateering and piracy emerges as a fascinating narrative that underscores the often blurred lines between legality and lawlessness on the immoderate seas. Privateering, a state-sanctioned form of maritime struggle, furnished a sanctioned framework for seizing enemy vessels in the route of times of conflict, at the same time as piracy, driven through character greed and ambition, frequently operated out of doors the bounds of legality. This financial ruin delves into the complex relationship between privateering and piracy, shedding slight at the motivations, strategies, and outcomes of those incredible but intertwined practices.

Privateering, often dubbed "gentlemanly warfare," placed its origins inside the age-old tradition of granting "letters of marque and reprisal." These files, issued thru a country's authority in some unspecified time inside the future of times of battle, prison private people or shipowners to equip vessels for the reason of capturing enemy ships and their shipment. Privateers, strolling with the backing in their respective governments, served as extensions of countrywide naval energy, the usage of their competencies to disrupt enemy exchange, weaken their adversaries, and bolster their very personal country's fortunes.

The enchantment of privateering lay in its ability for income. Captured ships and their cargoes have been regularly supplied, with the proceeds shared some of the group, shipowners, and the government issuing the letter of marque. This economic incentive attracted not most effective professional sailors however additionally enterprising human beings searching out to capitalize at the chaos of battle. The Atlantic global in a few unspecified time within the future of the 17th and 18th centuries witnessed a surge in privateering hobby, as colonial powers vied for dominance and manage of useful alternate routes.

However, the street amongst privateering and piracy have grow to be regularly a thin one. During instances of peace, privateers faced the challenge of transitioning from sanctioned warfare to valid maritime activities. Some privateers, pushed by means of the use of a lust for riches and the fun of the open sea, decided on to preserve their moves as pirates, seizing vessels no matter nationality or legality. This transition changed into now not commonly seamless, and a few governments struggled to rein in their as fast as-sanctioned privateers who had grew to turn out to be to piracy.

Pirates, frequently dubbed "enemies of all mankind," operated with a experience of independence that set them apart from the kingdom-sanctioned privateers. While privateers adhered to precise guidelines and policies mentioned in their letters of marque, pirates operated without such constraints, answering only to their very non-public dreams and codes of behavior. This lawlessness made pirates desires of naval government and legitimate privateers alike, as they posed a danger to each state pastimes and maritime trade.

Despite the difference amongst privateering and piracy, the 2 practices have been closely associated in the maritime global. During times of warfare, the street between sanctioned privateering and unchecked piracy need to emerge as blurry, with privateers venturing into ambiguous waters. The success of privateers often trusted the identical navigational capabilities, techniques, and weaponry as their pirate contrary numbers. This shared records allowed pirates to transition to privateering and vice versa, depending on the moving tides of geopolitics.

The line among privateering and piracy regularly came into sharp treatment for the duration of the transitions from war to peace. Governments could battle to govern the moves of privateers who, with out a smooth enemy to cause, could in all likelihood flip to piracy to sustain their livelihoods. This phenomenon highlighted the complicated relationship between character ambition, usa pursuits, and the converting dynamics of maritime conflict.

The narratives of privateering and piracy offer a window into the complicated net of human motivations, economic pastimes, and political machinations that formed the maritime panorama. As country-sanctioned privateers navigated the pleasant line amongst conflict and greed, pirates roamed the seas, difficult the norms of society and leaving their mark on records. The memories of these intertwined however notable practices maintain to captivate imaginations, reminding us of the complexities of human conduct within the ever-changing theater of the open sea.

Chapter 4: The Pirate Round

In the maritime chronicles of piracy, a captivating bankruptcy unfolds as pirates venture beyond the acquainted waters of the Atlantic and Caribbean to embark on an impressive odyssey referred to as the "Pirate Round." This audacious path led pirates to the faraway and great geographical areas of the Indian Ocean, wherein they sought new horizons, wealthy spoils, and the appeal of uncharted territories. The Pirate Round stands as a testomony to the pirates' insatiable thirst for adventure and riches, similarly to their functionality to comply to the moving tides of opportunity.

The origins of the Pirate Round may be traced to the early 18th century while pirates began to appearance past the acquainted routes of the West Indies for smooth targets and untapped resources. The Indian Ocean, with its thriving alternate routes connecting Europe, Africa, and Asia, emerged as a tantalizing tour spot for marauders in search of a alternate of environment and the functionality for extra rewards. As naval powers within the Atlantic intensified their efforts to suppress piracy, pirates observed the Indian Ocean's substantial expanse to be a steady haven in which they'll perform with relative impunity.

The Pirate Round's path turned into no longer constant; it meandered thru the Indian Ocean's labyrinthine network of sea routes, buying and selling ports, and coastal settlements. Pirates commenced their adventure in the Atlantic, frequently starting from ports in the Americas or the Caribbean. The Cape of Good Hope, on the southern tip of Africa, marked a great waypoint as pirates transitioned from the Atlantic to the Indian Ocean, navigating the treacherous waters around the Cape before setting their factors of hobby at the Indian subcontinent and past.

One of the maximum well-known pirates related to the Pirate Round became Captain Bartholomew Roberts, often known as "Black Bart." In 1719, Roberts launched proper right into a voyage that took him from the coast of West Africa to the Indian Ocean. His audacious capture of the ship "Great Mohammed" off the coast of Madagascar have come to be a pivotal 2d that signaled the appearance of the pirates within the Indian Ocean. Roberts and his institution went right now to plunder numerous vessels, amassing riches and solidifying their popularity as bold pirates.

The pirate haven of Madagascar, specifically the island of Sainte-Marie, have come to be a applicable hub for pirates working inside the Indian Ocean. Pirates used the island as a base to rest, refit their vessels, and divide their spoils. The island's an extended way off location and relatively lax governance allowed pirates to operate with a diploma of freedom not located in one of a type areas. They shaped free alliances and engaged in piracy at the excessive seas, preying on ships belonging to European colonial powers and Asian trading vessels.

The Pirate Round's attraction lay now not satisfactory in the promise of riches but also in the journey of exploring new territories and encountering severa cultures. Pirates encountered a myriad of challenges, from navigating unusual waters to clashing with community naval forces and rival pirate crews. The Indian Ocean, with its severa array of cultures and buying and selling hubs, supplied pirates with new research and opportunities for cultural trade.

As the Pirate Round received momentum, it drew the attention of the naval powers that held pastimes within the Indian Ocean. The British, French, Dutch, and Portuguese naval forces, often tasked with defensive their very very very own pursuits and change routes, engaged in fierce clashes with the pirates. The pirates, but, were no longer without problems deterred and hired their cunning strategies and intimate knowledge of the region's geography to save you capture and keep their plunder.

The Pirate Round, while marked with the resource of manner of bold exploits and unexpected encounters, sooner or later confronted demanding conditions that brought this era of piracy to a near. The growing naval presence inside the Indian Ocean, combined with rivalries among pirate crews and converting geopolitical dynamics, contributed to the decline of the Pirate Round. Pirates started out out to disperse, some returning to the Atlantic, others retiring, and a few going thru seize or loss of life at the arms of naval authorities.

The Pirate Round's legacy endures as a testament to the pirates' resourcefulness, adaptability, and insatiable starvation for journey. The Indian Ocean, as quickly as and uncharted realm, have emerge as a theater of maritime bold that showcased the pirates' capability to navigate the unknown and task the popularity quo. The recollections of the Pirate Round, complete of formidable raids, complicated alliances, and encounters with new cultures, preserve to captivate imaginations and remind us of the timeless attraction of the open sea.

Port Royal: Playground of Pirates

In the annals of pirate facts, few locations maintain the attraction and infamy of Port Royal, a bustling and lawless Caribbean port that have grow to be a haven for pirates, privateers, and people searching out a life beyond the regulations of society. Nestled on the southern coast of Jamaica, Port Royal emerged as a raucous den of iniquity for the duration of the Golden Age of Piracy, a place in which maritime outlaws and adventurers located shelter, camaraderie, and opportunity amidst the chaos of the high seas.

Port Royal's upward thrust to prominence changed into closely related to the growth of European colonial powers within the Caribbean within the direction of the 17th century. Initially set up via the use of the Spanish as a protecting outpost, Port Royal fell underneath English control in 1655 even as British forces captured Jamaica from the

Spanish. The strategic place of the port, positioned at the entrance to the Kingston Harbor, made it a extraordinary base for British naval operations and a hub for change within the place.

However, Port Royal's transformation proper right right into a pirate haven become speedy and dramatic. The port's lax governance, a ways off vicinity, and proximity to the main shipping routes of the Spanish Main made it an appealing destination for sailors looking for to break out the clutches of naval authorities and pursue lives of plunder and journey. Port Royal's fast increase and reputation as a den of vice drew a motley group of sailors, merchants, pirates, and prostitutes, growing a risky combination that described the man or woman of the port.

The taverns, brothels, and gambling houses of Port Royal bustled with interest, incomes the port the moniker "the wickedest metropolis inside the worldwide." The port's residents, cited for their debauchery and defiance of societal norms, reveled in a existence marked via way of extra and lawlessness. The spirit of anarchy and freedom that permeated Port Royal attracted pirates who sought to forge their very non-public destinies, untethered with the useful resource of the restraints of traditional society.

The presence of pirates and privateers have turn out to be an crucial a part of Port Royal's identification. The port's governor, Sir Henry Morgan, himself a former privateer have end up pirate, embodied the complicated courting amongst valid authority and piracy. Morgan's audacious exploits, consisting of the daring raid on Panama, earned him a recognition as a mythical figure in pirate lore. His have an impact on prolonged past his man or woman accomplishments, shaping Port Royal's popularity as a hub of maritime daring and opportunity.

The earthquake of 1692, a cataclysmic event that rocked Port Royal, marked a turning difficulty in its history. The city, recognised for its decadence and prosperity, modified into in huge component destroyed, with a bargain of its infrastructure sinking beneath the ocean. The catastrophe become seen with the resource of many as divine retribution for the town's sins, and the occasion served as a photograph of the fleeting nature of earthly pleasures.

While the earthquake devastated Port Royal, it did not mark the end of piracy or its legacy. The tales of Port Royal's lawless days and its association with piracy preserve to captivate imaginations, drawing vacationers and information enthusiasts to the remnants of the as soon as-thriving port. Today, Port Royal stands as a testomony to the audacity of folks who dared to defy societal norms and task the boundaries of civilization. The spirit of journey, freedom, and upward push up that described Port Royal's golden technology lives on within the memories of its populace, each infamous and forgotten, who left an indelible mark on the pages of pirate statistics.

Henry Morgan: From Privateer to Pirate

The existence and legacy of Sir Henry Morgan, a decide of each admiration and controversy, epitomize the complicated interaction amongst privateering and piracy in some unspecified time inside the future of the Golden Age of Piracy. From his humble beginnings in Wales to his bold exploits in the Caribbean, Morgan's transformation from a valid privateer to a notorious pirate shows the fluid nature of maritime warfare and the moving allegiances that defined this tumultuous technology.

Born in 1635 in Llanrumney, Wales, Henry Morgan's early years supplied little indication of the notorious career he might later embody. As a young man, he embarked on a adventure to the New World, arriving in Barbados in 1655. It became right here that he encountered the arena of privateering, a country-sanctioned shape of battle that allowed humans to attack enemy vessels and settlements in some unspecified time in the future of times of struggle. Morgan's abilities as a leader and his audacious technique to battle quick caught the attention of the British authorities.

Morgan's upward push to prominence got here in 1668 while he changed into commissioned as a privateer by way of Jamaican Governor Thomas Modyford. Tasked with harassing Spanish colonies and ships inside the Caribbean, Morgan's bold strategies and strategic acumen brought him achievement and fame. His audacious raid on the closely fortified town of Portobelo in gift-day Panama, a hub of Spanish change and wealth, earned him each riches and notoriety. This raid validated Morgan's willingness to have interaction in bold ventures that yielded massive rewards.

Yet, the road among privateering and piracy became often a thin one. Morgan's popularity for brutality and push aside for civilian lives drew criticism even inside the British colonial popularity quo. His participation in the sacking of the town of Maracaibo, Venezuela, in addition fueled accusations of his descent into piracy. Despite those allegations, Morgan's reputation and connections shielded him from severe results, and he persisted to feature beneath the British flag.

In 1671, Morgan released into his most notorious day journey: the raid on Panama City. This audacious undertaking aimed to capture one of the most wealthy towns in the Spanish Main, seemed for its opulence and strategic significance. The raid emerge as marked thru way of ruthless violence and the looting of the city, cementing Morgan's popularity as a fearsome and ruthless commander. The spoils from this raid had been big, however in addition they solidified Morgan's developing notoriety as a pirate.

The British crown's reaction to Morgan's moves have become mixed. While some officials lauded his successes and rewarded him with appointments, others had been uneasy approximately his strategies and the tensions his moves stirred with the Spanish. By the past due 1670s, the British authorities sought to distance itself from Morgan's sports, and he become ultimately arrested and sent to England to face costs for his conduct.

Despite his fall from grace, Morgan controlled to avoid excessive consequences for his actions. He turn out to be acquitted of prices and, astonishingly, become knighted through manner of the usage of King Charles II in 1674. However, his later years were marred via way of the usage of contamination, and he died in relative obscurity in Jamaica in 1688.

Henry Morgan's legacy is a mix of heroism and infamy, reflecting the difficult dynamics of the pirate international all through his time. He transitioned from a valid privateer to a pirate whose audacity and ruthlessness added him every riches and notoriety. His legacy endures as a reminder of the complexities of the Golden Age of Piracy, in which the road amongst sanctioned struggle and criminal employer may be blurred, and wherein people like Morgan navigated a shifting moral landscape to pursue their non-public goals and dreams.

Chapter 5: The Notorious Captain Kidd

Among the pantheon of legendary pirates, Captain William Kidd stands as a determine of intrigue, controversy, and enigma. His story, steeped in mystery and allegations of piracy, captures the essence of the Golden Age of Piracy and the complex dynamics of maritime lawlessness and u . S . Pursuits. Born in Scotland in 1645, Kidd's adventure from privateer to pirate captain to an accused felon embodies the complexities of a global wherein the limits amongst legality and crook hobby have been often blurred.

Kidd's childhood come to be marked with the resource of a desire for achievement and recognition. He ventured to the New World, in the end settling in New York City. His early endeavors covered running as a provider corporation and privateer, acquiring the patronage of influential figures in colonial society. Kidd's preliminary foray into privateering end up characterized by way of his provider on vessels commissioned to defend English pursuits in opposition to

French and Spanish competitors. He earned a reputation as a skilled sailor and leader, gaining the accept as genuine with of people who supported him.

In 1696, Kidd secured a charge from King William III to command the supply "Adventure Galley." His project emerge as to pursue and seize pirates who menaced the trade routes of the Indian Ocean and the Red Sea. However, the undertaking's actual nature may additionally need to rapid be mired in controversy and conflicting pursuits. Kidd struggled to find out pirates to capture, and as his frustrations grew, he have emerge as to taking pictures provider provider vessels in a determined attempt to salvage his task's success.

It end up in some unspecified time in the future of this era that the lines among privateering and piracy have end up increasingly more blurred. Kidd's actions, pushed through way of a combination of desperation and monetary pressures, converted him from a legitimate privateer to a pirate captain whose strategies and goals commenced out to resemble the ones of the very criminals he had were given all the manner down to recognize. His capture of the Quedagh Merchant, a supply of Indian basis, marked a turning element in his popularity, as accusations of piracy and brutality started out to circulate.

As records of Kidd's moves reached England, his patronage waned, and he decided himself increasingly more remoted. His move returned to the Caribbean turned into fraught with hazard, as naval government sought to recognize him for piracy. In 1699, Kidd have emerge as captured and transported to England, in which he faced trial for his movements. The trial itself become marred through political intrigue, conflicting memories, and allegations of corruption. Kidd's case captured the overall public's creativeness, fundamental to his conviction and eventual execution in 1701.

Kidd's legacy is a complicated tapestry of conflicting narratives and interpretations. While his trial and execution have been marked with the aid of way of controversy, his name have turn out to be synonymous with piracy within the famous imagination. The discovery of a cache of buried treasure associated with Kidd fueled legends of hidden riches and treasure maps, adding an air of mystery to his story.

The real quantity of Kidd's piracy stays a topic of discussion among historians. Some argue that his movements have been in huge part original with the aid of the pressures of his undertaking and the changing dynamics of maritime war. Others contend that he did truely end up a pirate, albeit reluctantly, as he navigated the uncertain waters of colonial politics, naval pursuits, and personal aims.

Captain Kidd's legacy endures as a picture of the complexities and contradictions that defined the Golden Age of Piracy. His story shows the tenuous stability between u . S . A

.-sanctioned moves and crook business enterprise, wherein the appeal of riches and the lure of journey regularly led human beings down paths that that they had not at the start supposed to tread. As a complicated and enigmatic determine, Captain Kidd's lifestyles maintains to captivate historians and lovers alike, reminding us of the complex narratives that lie beneath the floor of pirate facts.

Pirates in Popular Culture

The photograph of the swashbuckling pirate, with a eye patch, a cutlass at their element, and a parrot on their shoulder, has ingrained itself deeply in popular lifestyle, transcending time and area. From ancient maritime recollections to fashionable blockbuster movies, pirates have captured the imagination of human beings throughout the region, turning into iconic figures that evoke a enjoy of journey, upward push up, and freedom. This financial disaster delves into the captivating relationship amongst pirates and well-known subculture, tracing the evolution in their portrayal and impact on literature, movie, television, and past.

Pirates have a long and storied data in literature, dating back to ancient civilizations. The earliest recollections of maritime raiders, which include the Phoenician and Greek pirates, laid the muse for the archetype of the pirate as a parent of lawlessness and intrigue. In the Middle Ages, the Viking raiders and their sagas perpetuated the idea of seafaring outlaws. However, it have emerge as at some stage in the Golden Age of Piracy that pirates truly captured the general public's creativeness.

The ebook of "A General History of the Pyrates" via way of Captain Charles Johnson in 1724 marked a turning component within the portrayal of pirates in literature. This influential artwork chronicled the lives of famous pirates on the facet of Blackbeard, Black Bart, and Calico Jack, weaving real sports with fictional elaborations. The ebook created a template for pirate stories that combined swashbuckling motion, treacherous sea voyages, and formidable escapades. The fulfillment of Johnson's book contributed to the romanticization of pirates, reworking them into big-than-life characters whose exploits have end up the stuff of legend.

In the arena of visible arts, pirates determined a home in illustrations and engravings that decorated the pages of books and newspapers. These vivid depictions similarly cemented the well-known photograph of pirates, with eye patches, tricorn hats, peg legs, and Jolly Roger flags becoming immediately recognizable symbols. The pirate aesthetic of rise up and adventure captured the spirit of a society craving for escapism and thrills.

The 19th century witnessed a surge in pirate-themed literature, as authors like Robert Louis Stevenson delivered iconic characters like Long John Silver in "Treasure Island." This novel solidified the various pirate tropes that still resonate these days, including buried treasure, thriller maps, and divided loyalties. Stevenson's paintings captured the essence of pirate lore, infusing it with a experience of ethical ambiguity and complexity that went beyond mere caricatures.

As the twentieth century dawned, the appearance of cinema added pirates to lifestyles in a state-of-the-art and colourful manner. Silent films like "The Black Pirate" (1926) and "Captain Blood" (1935) transported audiences into the immoderate seas and grand adventures. Errol Flynn's portrayal of Captain Blood marked a defining 2nd in pirate cinema, putting the level for the swashbuckling heroes that would have a look at.

The 21st century has visible a resurgence of pirate fascination, fueled via films like "Pirates of the Caribbean," which brought Captain Jack Sparrow as a charismatic however morally ambiguous pirate. These movies mixed historic idea with supernatural elements, growing a tool that resonated with modern audiences. The recognition of those films expanded piracy to new heights of world recognition, turning Captain Jack Sparrow into a protracted lasting popular lifestyle icon.

Television series like "Black Sails" and video video video games like "Assassin's Creed IV: Black Flag" have similarly contributed to the iconic enchantment of pirates, exploring their lives, motivations, and the complicated realities of their global. The net age has allowed for the spread of pirate folklore, historical research, and modern expression, enabling enthusiasts to attach, communicate, and rejoice all subjects pirate-associated.

Pirates' have an impact on extends past amusement, infiltrating fashion, paintings, track, or maybe politics. The image of the pirate flag, the Jolly Roger, has come to be synonymous with rebellion and anti-repute quo sentiment. Pirate-themed merchandise, from apparel to accessories, remains a famous fashion, reflecting the timeless enchantment of the pirate aesthetic.

In end, the depiction of pirates in well-known culture is a testament to their enduring mystique and fascination. From historical legends to cutting-edge blockbusters, pirates have maintained a stronghold in the collective imagination, embodying the spirit of journey, defiance, and the look for freedom. As prolonged due to the fact the open sea calls to the human spirit, pirates will hold to navigate the seas of well-known subculture, leaving an indelible mark on literature, cinema, and the wider landscape of entertainment.

The End of the Golden Age

The curtain become drawing to a near on the swashbuckling era that had grow to be referred to as the Golden Age of Piracy. The recollections of bold sea raids, treasure hunts, and big-than-lifestyles characters were giving way to a changing worldwide order and moving dynamics that would in the end sign the surrender of an era that had captured the area's imagination.

By the early 18th century, the maritime panorama have emerge as present process great changes. The as fast as-thriving empires that had fueled the sports activities activities of pirates have been asserting their dominance and cracking down on piracy with renewed electricity. Colonial powers, collectively with Britain, France, and Spain, commenced to appearance pirates no longer high-quality as threats to exchange but as enemies of the united states of america. The Treaty of Utrecht in 1713, which ended the War of the Spanish Succession, marked a turning component, with many governments explicitly prohibiting piracy and privateering.

The enforcement of anti-piracy measures delivered large strain upon pirates, pushing them to the fringes of the maritime worldwide. The decline of the pirate havens, such as Nassau in the Bahamas, further constrained their operations. Pirates who as soon as loved relative freedom decided themselves more and more remoted and hunted, struggling to hold their manner of lifestyles amidst the developing naval presence and tighter control of exchange routes.

Naval authorities, eager to suppress piracy, launched massive campaigns to eliminate pirates and their hideouts. Legendary pirates like Blackbeard and Charles Vane met their demise at the hands of naval forces. The British authorities, particularly, took a strong stance in competition to piracy, the usage of ruthless measures to seize and execute pirates, as exemplified via the notorious "Pirate Roundup" of 1718 in the Bahamas.

Technological improvements also completed a feature inside the decline of piracy. The introduction of quicker and extra effective naval vessels, armed with stepped forward weaponry, enabled naval forces to pursue pirates with greater basic performance. Additionally, the spread of accurate navigational equipment and advanced maritime information made it an increasing number of hard for pirates to prevent seize and navigate uncharted waters.

Economic shifts also contributed to the decline of piracy. As worldwide trade routes have emerge as extra established and exchange have emerge as lots much less beneficial, the enchantment of piracy waned. The decline of piracy become similarly exacerbated via the increase of possibility opportunities for humans looking for wealth and journey. The exploration and colonization of recent territories, collectively with the increase of prison carrier provider ventures, supplied new avenues for folks who as quickly as would possibly have have come to be to piracy.

The final nail inside the coffin of the Golden Age of Piracy got here with the developing cooperation amongst colonial powers to suppress piracy. The coordinated efforts of Britain, France, and special countries introduced approximately joint naval patrols and the sharing of intelligence, making it exceedingly hard for pirates to interrupt out justice. The Pirate Round, as quickly as a formidable course of adventure, have come to be a risky lure as naval forces patrolled key chokepoints and captured pirate vessels.

As the 18th century superior, the as quickly as-effective pirate crews splintered and disbanded, their leaders captured or killed, their ships scuttled or repurposed for valid endeavors. The romanticized photograph of the pirate started out to offer way to a harsher truth of quick justice and an evolving worldwide order. The swashbuckling adventures that had captured the general public's imagination dwindled into data, leaving at the back of a legacy that might be immortalized in literature, art work, and well-known lifestyle.

In cease, the give up of the Golden Age of Piracy marked the last of a financial ruin in maritime statistics that had captivated the arena with memories of riot, adventure, and lawlessness on the immoderate seas. The decline of piracy have become driven with the aid of a confluence of things, from converting geopolitics to technological upgrades and evolving economic landscapes. While the generation of pirates had come to an give up, their legacy endured to stay on, inspiring endless memories, movies, and imaginations for generations to go again.

Chapter 6: The Pirate Republic Of Nassau

In the annals of pirate lore, few memories are as fascinating because the rise and fall of the Pirate Republic of Nassau. Nestled inside the idyllic waters of the Bahamas, Nassau emerged as a lawless haven wherein pirates ought to forge their very private destinies, free from the regulations of colonial government and societal norms. This chapter delves into the captivating statistics of the Pirate Republic, exploring its origins, governance, and last loss of existence.

The origins of the Pirate Republic of Nassau can be traced returned to the early 18th century, at some diploma in the heyday of the Golden Age of Piracy. The Bahamas, a reasonably populated and some distance flung archipelago, supplied an excellent backdrop for pirates trying to find a steady harbor to rest, refit their vessels, and divide their spoils. The island of New Providence, home to the town of Nassau, has become a focal point for pirates drawn via using the promise of freedom and riches.

Nassau's transformation proper proper right into a pirate haven changed into catalyzed with the beneficial useful resource of the void left by the usage of British government. The Bahamas, as speedy as a British colonial outpost, had been in large factor ignored and abandoned the vacuum of en Chapter ergy created an opportunity for pirates to seize manipulate of the island and installation their non-public society. Pirates from first rate corners of the arena, which includes the Caribbean, Africa, and Europe, converged on Nassau, developing a numerous and dynamic network.

The Pirate Republic of Nassau modified into no longer a conventional republic in the traditional experience; it lacked a formal authorities form and sizeable authority. Instead, the pirates operated below a code of behavior referred to as the "Articles of Agreement" or "Pirate Code." This unwritten however universally acquainted set of recommendations cited guidelines for the manner pirates need to manipulate themselves, percentage spoils, and hold order inside their ranks.

One of the critical aspect figures inside the installed order of the Pirate Republic changed into the notorious pirate captain Benjamin Hornigold. Hornigold identified the capability of Nassau as a pirate stronghold and led raids to seize the island from British forces. Under his control, Nassau converted from a sleepy outpost to a bustling hub of maritime interest. The pirates constructed forts, set up a rudimentary criminal device, or maybe elected officers to supervise their affairs.

The Pirate Code, despite the fact that no longer formalized in a written file, pondered the pirates' desire for a degree of order and equity inside their society. The code emphasised necessities which incorporates identical branch of plunder, safety of institution people, and prohibitions in the direction of playing and stopping on board. The democratic nature of the code allowed pirates, no matter rank or beginning, to have a voice in selection-making and dispute desire.

The Pirate Republic of Nassau flourished for a rather quick duration, from about 1706 to 1718. During this time, Nassau have end up a hub of piracy and trade, attracting traders and sailors looking for to benefit from the pirates' illicit sports activities sports. The presence of pirates injected power into the neighborhood financial machine, as taverns, brothels, and organizations catered to their needs.

However, the Pirate Republic's days had been numbered. The developing naval presence and efforts thru colonial powers to suppress piracy posed a wonderful risk to Nassau's lifestyles. In 1718, Britain launched a advertising marketing campaign to quell piracy inside the Bahamas, culminating in a naval blockade and the seize of many pirate vessels. The as quickly as-effective Pirate Republic fell, and Nassau emerge as reclaimed with the resource of British forces.

The legacy of the Pirate Republic of Nassau endures as a testomony to the pirates' audacity and functionality to create a society that operated outdoor the installed norms of the time. The technology of pirate governance in Nassau showcased the pirates' functionality for enterprise, cooperation, and version. While the Pirate Republic became quick-lived, its memory lives on inside the recollections of mythical pirates, the artifacts decided on the sea floor, and the iconic fascination with an era wherein pirates in short held sway over their personal future.

Pirates in the New World

The New World, with its massive uncharted waters, untamed landscapes, and promise of riches, have end up a haven for pirates searching out journey, plunder, and a danger to redefine their lives. The 16th to 18th centuries witnessed a surge in pirate interest all through the Atlantic, as European powers multiplied their empires and mounted colonies in the Americas. The attraction of the

New World, coupled with its complex geopolitical landscape, created fertile ground for piracy to flourish.

As European international places vied for dominance in the New World, the waters surrounding the Americas teemed with merchant vessels encumbered with precious items. The Caribbean, mainly, emerged as a hotbed of pirate hobby due to its strategic area as a crossroads for change routes amongst Europe, Africa, and the Americas. Pirates capitalized on the chaotic situation inside the location, wherein rival empires, pirates, and indigenous peoples all intersected.

Pirates in the New World came from numerous backgrounds, collectively with sailors, former privateers, escaped slaves, and upset colonists. Many sought safe haven inside the New World to escape the strictures of society or the repercussions in their beyond actions. The New World supplied them with a clean canvas on which they may create new identities and pursue wealth and freedom.

One of the earliest examples of pirates within the New World were the "Buccaneers" who operated inside the Caribbean in some unspecified time in the future of the seventeenth century. These marauders, frequently of French or English beginning, were a mixture of hunters, adventurers, and pirates. They set up settlements on islands like Tortuga and Hispaniola, in which they lived off the land, hunted wild game, and plundered Spanish ships. The Buccaneers' techniques regularly blurred the strains between piracy and country-sanctioned privateering.

The Buccaneers' sports activities ultimately gave manner to the Golden Age of Piracy, a duration characterised by using using swashbuckling captains, formidable raids, and tales of buried treasure. The notorious pirate havens of Nassau and Port Royal inside the Caribbean have emerge as epicenters of pirate interest. These lawless ports attracted pirates who sought shelter, camaraderie, and the opportunity to build up wealth through acts of piracy.

Pirates inside the New World evolved precise strategies to navigate the difficult maritime surroundings. They employed rapid and nimble vessels called "sloops" and "frigates," letting them outrun big naval ships. Pirates used their intimate expertise of the coastal geography to their benefit, utilizing hidden coves, shallow waters, and labyrinthine passages to influence easy of capture and ambush unsuspecting prey.

The New World additionally introduced pirates face-to-face with numerous cultures and societies. Pirates regularly interacted with indigenous populations, from time to time forming alliances and exclusive times clashing in violent confrontations. These interactions brought complexity to the pirate narrative, highlighting the cultural exchanges and conflicts that fashioned the maritime worldwide of the time.

The decline of piracy in the New World modified into brought about by means of manner of a selection of factors. The developing naval presence of colonial powers, the developing cooperation amongst international locations to suppress piracy, and the transformation of the New World from untamed frontier to installation colonies all contributed to the decline. By the mid-18th century, piracy's heyday had exceeded, and the swashbuckling technology commenced out to vanish into facts.

The legacy of pirates within the New World lives on within the memories, legends, and artifacts that maintain to captivate our creativeness. The pirates' exploits and audacious adventures live a testament to human resilience, adaptability, and the pursuit of freedom and wealth. The New World furnished a backdrop for their ambitious escapades, growing a wealthy tapestry of history that shows the complexities of a swiftly changing world and the indomitable spirit of people who dared to sail its uncharted waters.

The Pursuit of Pirate Hunters

The battle among pirates and those tasked with their capture, the pirate hunters, is a gripping narrative that spans centuries and oceans. From the rise of piracy at some stage in the Golden Age to the eventual decline of their lawless reign, pirate hunters performed a important position in preserving maritime order and safeguarding alternate routes. This financial catastrophe explores the daring pastimes, techniques, and conflicts that defined the pursuit of pirate hunters.

Pirate hunters emerged as a reaction to the escalating risk of piracy that plagued the seas. Colonial powers and governments identified the need to defend their provider issuer vessels and exchange hobbies from the scourge of pirates. Naval officials, privateers grew to end up lawful enforcers, and devoted crews composed the ranks of these pirate hunters. Their assignment changed into to discover, engage, and understand pirates who disrupted exchange and threatened the stability of the seas.

The pursuit of pirate hunters end up characterized thru audacity and ambitious. Pirate-infested waters required unconventional strategies and rapid motion. Pirate hunters operated from well-armed vessels, often outfitted with superior firepower and advanced navigational gear. These vessels had been built for speed, letting them pursue and interact pirate ships with agility and precision. Pirate hunters often hired misleading strategies, disguising their vessels to lull pirates into a fake feel of safety in advance than revealing their actual motive.

One of the maximum well-known pirate hunters of the generation have turn out to be Woodes Rogers, a former privateer who've turn out to be appointed as the governor of the Bahamas. Rogers turned into tasked with suppressing piracy in the location and taken the pirate haven of Nassau under British control. He initiated a marketing marketing campaign to provide pardons to pirates who surrendered and decrease again to a lawful existence. This approach effectively divided the pirate community, as a few pirates selected to clearly get hold of the amnesty, on the equal time as others persisted their piratical pursuits.

The pursuit of pirate hunters prolonged past the seas and into the criminal justice tool. Pirate hunters often captured pirates and brought them to trial, looking for justice for his or her crimes. Trials of pirates had been regularly public spectacles, serving as a deterrent to others considering a life of piracy. Notable trials, which consist of the trial of Bartholomew Roberts' organization people, showcased the lengths to which authorities have been inclined to visit suppress piracy.

The pursuit of pirate hunters have become not without its demanding conditions. Pirates had been creative and adept at evasion. They regularly navigated treacherous waters and used their statistics of coastlines and hidden coves to elude capture. Some pirate hunters resorted to unconventional procedures, together with infiltrating pirate crews undercover to collect intelligence or launching surprise attacks under the cover of darkness.

The final decline of piracy become caused via using a mixture of things, which includes the concerted efforts of pirate hunters. The stepped forward naval presence, the set up order of anti-piracy prison guidelines and regulations, and the decline of pirate havens all played a role in suppressing piracy. The shift in international politics and the transition from a maritime international dominated through pirates to at least one dominated thru colonial powers signaled the stop of an era.

The pursuit of pirate hunters remains a charming element of pirate data, highlighting the complex dance between law enforcement and those who sought to make the most the lawlessness of the seas. The stories of legendary pirate hunters and their daring exploits hold to encourage memories of heroism, foxy, and resolution. The legacy of the pursuit of pirate hunters is a reminder of the long-lasting conflict to keep order on the excessive seas and the indomitable spirit of folks that risked their lives to maintain pirates to justice.

Chapter 7: Famous Naval Battles Against Pirates

The annals of maritime records are punctuated with dramatic and harrowing naval battles waged toward pirates. These clashes on the excessive seas marked important moments inside the war to suppress piracy and guard maritime exchange routes. This financial ruin delves into some of the maximum famous naval battles fought closer to pirates, showcasing the bravery, techniques, and strategic maneuvering that customary the effects of these encounters.

One of the earliest and maximum outstanding naval battles within the direction of pirates have turn out to be the Battle of Ocracoke Inlet in 1718. It pitted the pirate Blackbeard and his deliver, the Queen Anne's Revenge, in competition to British naval forces led via Lieutenant Robert Maynard. The battle took place off the coast of North Carolina, and Blackbeard's vessel engaged Maynard's ships in a fierce confrontation. After hours of immoderate fight, Maynard's forces managed to board the Queen Anne's Revenge and engage in close to-region fight. In a dramatic showdown, Blackbeard met his lack of existence, and his dying marked a massive blow to piracy inside the area.

In 1720, the infamous pirate Bartholomew Roberts, referred to as "Black Bart," engaged in a fierce warfare in competition to the British Royal Navy ship HMS Swallow off the coast of West Africa. Roberts, who had risen to prominence as one of the maximum a success pirates of his time, changed into focused thru the British army with the intention to suppress his activities. The conflict resulted in Roberts' dying, however his dedication and defiance left an indelible mark on pirate lore.

The warfare among the pirate Charles Vane and the pirate hunter Captain Jonathan Barnet in 1718 off the coast of the Bahamas exemplified the complex dynamics of maritime conflict. Vane, notorious for his ruthless strategies, modified into cornered thru Barnet's forces. Vane's vessel, the Ranger, have end up outnumbered and outgunned, and he in the end surrendered after a prolonged fight. Vane's capture confirmed the effect of coordinated efforts to suppress piracy.

The conflict among pirate hunters and the pirate stronghold of Nassau in 1718 marked a turning element within the conflict in opposition to piracy within the Caribbean. British naval forces, led by way of manner of Captain Woodes Rogers, launched an attack on Nassau, which had emerge as a hub for pirate hobby. The a hit seize of Nassau allowed Rogers to set up British control over the island, efficaciously finishing its function as a pirate haven and disrupting pirate operations inside the region.

The Battle of Cape Lopez in 1722 have grow to be a sizeable engagement among British naval forces and pirate vessels running off the coast of West Africa. The British naval supply HMS Swallow, commanded through Captain

Chaloner Ogle, engaged a fleet of pirate vessels led through Bartholomew Roberts. The battle modified into excessive, with both additives using cunning strategies and maneuvering to benefit the higher hand. Despite their numerical disadvantage, Ogle's forces managed to defeat the pirates, sinking or shooting severa of their ships.

The Battle of New Orleans in 1815, some years after the peak of the Golden Age of Piracy, showcased the persevering with war in opposition to piracy even as the generation waned. The infamous pirate Jean Lafitte, who had set up a base in Louisiana, located himself at odds with American forces in some unspecified time in the future of the War of 1812. Lafitte's privateer fleet and his expert techniques played a essential function in defensive New Orleans from British invasion. The conflict highlighted the complicated allegiances and converting roles of former pirates in times of war.

These famous naval battles closer to pirates underscore the excessive-stakes nature of the conflict to suppress piracy and keep maritime order. The clashes amongst pirate hunters and pirates, marked via manner of bravery, cunning, and strategic acumen, left an extended-lasting effect on the historic narrative of piracy. These battles feature a reminder of the worrying conditions confronted by using manner of the use of the ones tasked with preventing piracy and the indomitable spirit of those who sought to protect the excessive seas from lawlessness and chaos.

Legends and Mythology of Pirates

The legacy of pirates extends a long manner beyond ancient facts, permeating the vicinity of legends and mythology. Throughout the some time, pirates have captivated the human creativeness, giving upward thrust to memories of formidable adventures, buried treasure, and enigmatic characters. This financial ruin delves into the wealthy tapestry of legends and mythology which have woven themselves across the determine of the pirate, from the Golden Age of Piracy to fashionable instances.

Pirate legends frequently blur the strains among fact and fiction, melding historical sports activities with gildings and innovative flourishes. The iconic image of the pirate, whole with eye patches, peg legs, and parrots, has end up an extended-lasting photo of lawlessness and journey. These exaggerated capabilities have emerge as so ingrained in popular subculture that they have got emerge as synonymous with piracy itself, no matter their historic accuracy.

The stories of buried treasure have fueled the imagination of generations, inspiring countless memories and adventures. The notion of pirates amassing massive fortunes and stashing them away in hidden coves or on remote islands has given upward thrust to the archetype of the treasure map, complete with "X marks the spot." While a few times of buried treasure are rooted in ancient sports activities, many are products of revolutionary storytelling which have taken on a life of their private.

One of the most famous pirate legends is that of Captain Kidd's buried treasure. Captain William Kidd, once a privateer became pirate hunter, changed into performed in 1701 for piracy and murder. In the years following his dying, rumors spread of his hidden treasure, prompting treasure hunters to embark on quests to discover it. While a few have claimed to locate remnants of his alleged treasure, the fact in the back of these tales stays elusive.

Chapter 8: Blackbeard

Edward Teach, famously called Blackbeard, have come to be one of the most infamous and feared pirates during the "Golden Age of Piracy" within the early 18th century. His life and exploits have grow to be mythical, and he is often depicted because the archetypal pirate with a fearsome look and a recognition for ruthlessness.

Early Life and Career:

Edward Teach changed into probably born around 1680 in Bristol, England, no matter the truth that information about his youngsters stay murky and speculative. He entered the maritime worldwide, to start with serving as a privateer in the course of Queen Anne's War (1702-1713). Privateers have been basically crook pirates, prison by means of governments to assault and plunder enemy vessels sooner or later of instances of battle.

Transformation into Blackbeard:

After the conflict, Teach have end up to piracy and began his infamous profession. He obtained the nickname "Blackbeard" due to his splendid appearance—prolonged, black beard, and gradual-burning fuses or hemp cords tucked into his beard, developing an intimidating and fearsome picture. During struggle, he must mild the fuses, enveloping his face in smoke and giving him an even more menacing appearance.

Command of the Queen Anne's Revenge:

Blackbeard's flagship turn out to be the Queen Anne's Revenge, a former French slave supply that he captured and organized with 40 weapons. This bold vessel have become a picture of terror in the Caribbean and along the American colonies' Atlantic coast.

Infamous Acts and Notoriety:

Blackbeard's popularity for cruelty and intimidation became cautiously cultivated. He can also tie gradual-burning fuses into his beard and slight them in the end of war, developing a demonic photo of smoke and hearth. This theatrical display changed into supposed to frighten his enemies into surrender without a combat.

One of Blackbeard's most infamous acts changed into the blockade of Charleston, South Carolina, in 1718. He captured numerous ships and held first-rate residents for ransom, developing panic and organising his dominance in the place.

The End of Blackbeard:

Blackbeard's reign of terror came to an cause November 1718. The British Royal Navy, under the command of Lieutenant Robert Maynard, engaged Blackbeard's fleet close to Ocracoke Island, North Carolina. After a fierce battle, Blackbeard changed into killed in movement, enduring a couple of gunshot wounds and sword cuts.

Maynard's forces captured Blackbeard's head, which come to be then displayed on the deliver's bowsprit as a caution to one of a kind pirates. This marked the surrender of Blackbeard's piratical career, even though his legend continued to growth in the centuries that accompanied.

Legacy and Folklore:

Blackbeard's legacy is deeply ingrained in maritime folklore and well-known manner of life. His ruthless strategies, specific appearance, and the thriller surrounding his childhood make a contribution to the iconic fascination along with his tale. Numerous books, films, and TV indicates have depicted the notorious pirate, immortalizing Blackbeard as a image of the Golden Age of Piracy.

Anne Bonny

Anne Bonny, a infamous female pirate, became a outstanding decide at some stage in the "Golden Age of Piracy" in the early 18th century. Her lifestyles is shrouded in thriller and legend, and he or she or he's remembered for her fearless and rebellious spirit in a male-dominated global of piracy.

Early Life:

Anne Bonny became born round 1702 in County Cork, Ireland, to William Cormac, a plantation proprietor, and his servant. Her own family emigrated to the American colonies at the same time as she become a infant. Growing up in the turbulent and lawless surroundings of the Caribbean, Anne was uncovered to the tough and adventurous lifestyles that could later outline her.

Connection to Piracy:

Anne Bonny's course to piracy started while she married a small-time pirate named James Bonny. However, she quick have become dissatisfied collectively together with her marriage and eloped with the infamous pirate Calico Jack (John Rackham) within the early 18th century. Together with Mary Read, every other girl pirate, Anne Bonny joined Calico Jack's team.

Pirate Adventures:

Calico Jack's team, which includes Anne Bonny and Mary Read, engaged in piracy inside the Caribbean waters. Anne Bonny became stated for her capacity with weapons, her fiery temperament, and her willingness to take part in the pirate life along the men. Legend has it that she should outdrink and outfight pretty some her male opposite numbers.

Capture and Trial:

In October 1720, Calico Jack's deliver emerge as captured with the aid of a British naval sloop led thru Captain Jonathan Barnet. Anne Bonny and Mary Read, the two lady pirates, fiercely resisted seize, even as maximum of the male crew individuals were too inebriated to combat. The girls were in the end overpowered and arrested.

Fate and Mystery:

Both Anne Bonny and Mary Read faced trial for piracy. During her trial, Anne Bonny's future took an sudden flip at the equal time as she observed that she end up pregnant. Her execution modified into postponed, and there aren't any ancient records confirming that she end up ever completed. Some money owed advocate that her father can also have secured her release, even as others claim she escaped from prison.

Legacy and Folklore:

Anne Bonny's life has turn out to be the stuff of legend, perpetuated with the useful useful resource of pirate folklore and famous life-style. Her tale has been romanticized in severa books, films, and songs. The photo of a fiery and fearless lady pirate hard societal norms has made her an iconic determine within the data of piracy.

In modern day years, there was renewed interest in Anne Bonny's existence, with historians and college college students re-inspecting historic information to break up reality from fiction. Despite the mystery surrounding her final destiny, Anne Bonny stays a picture of woman empowerment and rebellion within the frequently-brutal international of piracy sooner or later of the Golden Age.

Bartholomew Roberts

Bartholomew Roberts, often called "Black Bart," modified into a Welsh pirate who acquired notoriety as one of the maximum successful and prolific pirates in the course of the "Golden Age of Piracy" in the early 18th century. His quick however impactful profession marked him as an exceptional pressure within the waters off the Americas and West Africa.

Early Life:

Born John Roberts in 1682 in Pembrokeshire, Wales, little is concept approximately his children. Roberts to begin with pursued a profession at sea, serving as a service issuer sailor. His lifestyles took a dramatic flip in 1719 while the ship he changed into aboard, the slave deliver Princess, modified into captured by means of the use of the pirate Howell Davis. Rather than resisting capture, Roberts joined Davis' institution, embarking on his path to piracy.

Rise to Prominence:

Roberts short rose thru the ranks inside the pirate network. Following Davis' death in a struggle with Portuguese forces off the coast of West Africa, Roberts grow to be elected because the contemporary captain with the resource of his fellow pirates. Known for his management talents, intelligence, and capability to speak more than one languages, Roberts accompanied the discover of "Commodore" and set out to carve his very personal legacy on the excessive seas.

Pirate Code and Discipline:

Roberts carried out a strict pirate code aboard his supply, the Royal Fortune, which have grow to be a version for unique pirate crews. The code blanketed policies about group conduct, distribution of plunder, and democratic preference-making. Roberts believed in preserving order and location among his organization, fostering a feel of harmony and cause.

Raiding and Plundering:

Under Roberts' command, the Royal Fortune have turn out to be a formidable strain inside the Atlantic and Indian Oceans. Roberts focused a massive form of vessels, along side service issuer ships, warships, and slavers. His audacity and foxy tactics allowed him to capture over 4 hundred ships at some stage in his piracy career, an incredible achievement in the records of piracy.

Naval Engagements:

Roberts' audacity extended to tough naval vessels of vital powers. In 1720, he engaged a fleet of Portuguese and British warships off the coast of West Africa in what have turn out to be called the Battle of Cape Lopez. Despite going via overwhelming odds, Roberts displayed tactical prowess, escaping the engagement with best minor damage to his ship.

Death and Legacy:

Bartholomew Roberts' existence as a pirate came to an abrupt give up on February 10, 1722, off the coast of Cape Lopez (present-day Gabon) on the equal time because the Royal Fortune changed into ambushed by way of the usage of a British naval squadron led with the beneficial aid of Captain Chaloner Ogle. Roberts fought valiantly however succumbed to his injuries. His loss of life marked the prevent of one of the maximum a hit pirate careers in information.

Roberts' legacy endures in pirate lore and maritime facts. His achievements, which encompass his top notch seize of ships and his effect on pirate governance, continue to be studied by manner of historians. The photo of Black Bart, wearing complex clothing, wielding multiple pistols, and embracing the romanticized notion of the pirate, remains a long-lasting photo of the Golden Age of Piracy.

Calico Jack (John Rackham)

Calico Jack, whose real name became John Rackham, turned into a infamous pirate who operated at a few level in the "Golden Age of Piracy" inside the early 18th century. He gained infamy now not superb for his crook activities however moreover for his association with well-known girl pirates, Anne Bonny and Mary Read. Calico Jack's short however colourful career left an indelible mark on the statistics of piracy.

Early Life:

John Rackham changed into likely born in the overdue 17th century in England. Little is concept about his youth, and he first appears in ancient statistics as a quartermaster aboard a British man-of-war during the War of Spanish Succession. Rackham became to piracy after the conflict, searching out the lure of wealth and journey on the excessive seas.

Rise to Captaincy:

Rackham's career as a pirate won momentum whilst he joined the crew of Charles Vane, every other infamous pirate. Eventually, Rackham became disillusioned with Vane's leadership and, in conjunction with unique discontented institution contributors, ousted him from command. Rackham took control of the supply, which he renamed the Revenge, and released into his non-public piratical endeavors.

Infamous Flag and Moniker:

Calico Jack earned his moniker from the calico garb he frequently wore, a great cloth that contributed to his flamboyant and recognizable look. His Jolly Roger, the pirate flag, featured a skull with crossed swords underneath it, symbolizing the pirate's willingness to combat to the loss of existence.

Association with Anne Bonny and Mary Read:

One of Calico Jack's most widespread contributions to pirate lore modified into his association with bold woman pirates, Anne Bonny and Mary Read. Both ladies dressed as men to cover their gender, and they accomplished energetic roles in the institution, contributing to the group's reputation for audacity and ferocity.

Pirate Exploits:

Calico Jack's piracy mainly centered on the waters of the Caribbean. His group engaged in acts of piracy, plundering carrier provider vessels and evading pursuit thru the usage of naval authorities. The audacious trio of Calico Jack, Anne Bonny, and Mary Read created a reputation that struck worry into the hearts of sailors and coastal groups.

Capture and Trial:

Calico Jack's piratical profession met its purpose October 1720 even as a British naval sloop, commanded through using Captain Jonathan Barnet, cornered the pirate supply in Jamaica. The employer, such as Anne Bonny and Mary Read, resisted arrest, but they have been ultimately captured. Calico Jack and his team had been taken to Jamaica for trial.

Execution and Legacy:

In November 1720, Calico Jack, at the facet of several participants of his group, faced trial in Spanish Town, Jamaica. Found responsible of piracy, they have been sentenced to hold. Calico Jack met his future at Gallows Point on November 17, 1720.

Calico Jack's legacy lives on in pirate folklore and famous way of lifestyles. His association with Anne Bonny and Mary Read, in addition to his brilliant flag and flamboyant apparel, have cemented his place within the annals of piracy. His brief-lived however impactful career stays a testament to the appeal and perils of a life at the immoderate seas at some stage in the Golden Age of Piracy.

Chapter 9: Captain Kidd

Captain William Kidd, regularly referred to as Captain Kidd, changed proper into a Scottish sailor and privateer grew to emerge as pirate who lived within the direction of the late 17th century. His life is marked thru a complicated and arguable legacy, as he transitioned from an amazing privateer commissioned through colonial powers to a infamous pirate hunted through the identical government.

Early Life and Privateering:

William Kidd became born in Greenock, Scotland, spherical 1645. Little is thought about his adolescence, however he began his maritime profession as a privateer in the course of the past due seventeenth century. Privateers were privately owned ships commissioned with the useful resource of governments in the direction of instances of conflict to attack enemy vessels and disrupt exchange.

Commission as a Privateer:

In 1695, Kidd secured a charge from the English authorities to captain the Adventure Galley, a privateer vessel. His venture turned into to fight piracy within the Indian Ocean and defend English ships from pirate assaults. However, his venture faced monetary annoying situations, and Kidd struggled to deliver collectively a group willing to address the harmful assignment.

Turn to Piracy:

As economic troubles set up, Kidd's team grew increasingly more pissed off, and he located himself in a difficult feature. Frustrated through using the lack of fulfillment in privateering, he grew to come to be to piracy. Kidd started out preying on ships no matter their nationality, and his popularity short shifted from that of a privateer to a infamous pirate.

Hunt for Kidd:

News of Kidd's piratical sports activities reached England, and he became a preferred man. The British East India Company and the Royal Navy initiated a hunt for Kidd, branding him a pirate and enemy of the Crown. Kidd's reputation as a pirate, however, remains debated amongst historians, with a few suggesting that he would possibly probable have persisted to motive satisfactory enemy vessels.

Capture and Trial:

In 1699, Kidd's piratical profession came to an forestall at the same time as he become captured off the coast of New England. He modified into taken to England, in which he faced a relatively publicized trial. Kidd vehemently denied the charges of piracy, claiming that his moves were consistent along with his genuine privateering charge. Nevertheless, he have become determined responsible of piracy and homicide.

Execution:

Captain Kidd grow to be hanged on May 23, 1701, at Execution Dock in Wapping, London.

His frame changed into left installing a gibbet alongside the Thames River as a warning to others who may also do not forget a existence of piracy. The macabre show served as a stark reminder of the effects looking for people who grew to end up to piracy.

Kidd's Buried Treasure:

The legend of Captain Kidd's buried treasure has captured the imaginations of human beings for centuries. Tales of hidden riches on islands and along coastlines have fueled numerous treasure hunts, however no massive proof of Kidd's buried treasure has ever been determined.

Legacy and Controversy:

Captain Kidd's legacy remains controversial. While some view him as a notorious pirate who betrayed his fee, others argue that his moves could have been a result of desperation and out of doors pressures. The legend of his buried treasure, whether or now not or now not actual or imagined, has contributed to the long-lasting fascination along along with his tale in famous manner of lifestyles.

Captain Kidd's life and the controversy surrounding his intentions live subjects of historic studies and hypothesis. The complicated narrative of a privateer have become pirate highlights the blurred traces amongst legality and unlawful hobby at some point of the tumultuous duration of maritime warfare and colonial enlargement within the overdue 17th century.

Henry Morgan

Henry Morgan, a Welsh privateer and later a pirate, emerged as one of the maximum notorious figures of the "Golden Age of Piracy" inside the path of the overdue seventeenth century. His exploits inside the Caribbean earned him every admiration and infamy, and his legacy has left an indelible mark on the records of piracy.

Early Life and Career:

Henry Morgan modified into born round 1635 in Llanrumney, Wales, right right into a quite modest information. Little is known approximately his children, but via the 1660s, he had ventured into the Caribbean as a part of the buccaneering expeditions. Initially serving as a privateer, Morgan became commissioned via the English authorities to attack and disrupt Spanish colonies and delivery all through the Second Anglo-Spanish War.

Buccaneering Exploits:

Morgan's early profession worried raiding Spanish settlements inside the Caribbean. He participated in expeditions towards the Spanish Main, collecting wealth and reputation via plundering towns like Porto Bello and Maracaibo. Morgan's ruthless techniques and strategic acumen acquired him decide on among his fellow privateers and earned him promotions inside their ranks.

Raid on Panama:

In 1670, Morgan led his maximum well-known and bold raid on Panama City, a key Spanish stronghold. The a fulfillment capture of the city introduced large wealth to Morgan and his institution, solidifying his reputation as a cunning and audacious leader. The raid on Panama is frequently taken into consideration one of the maximum massive sports of Morgan's career.

Transition to Piracy:

Despite his service to the English crown, Morgan's moves an increasing number of blurred the street among privateering and outright piracy. His raids have come to be greater opportunistic, targeting every Spanish and non-Spanish vessels, which drew the ire of European powers. In 1671, Morgan become arrested and taken once more to England to face fees of piracy.

Royal Pardon and Knighthood:

To the marvel of many, together with Morgan himself, he have end up no longer nice acquitted of the costs but changed into moreover knighted through King Charles II. Morgan's newfound recognition as a knight contemplated the ambiguous relationship amongst privateering and piracy at some point of this period. He turn out to be in the end appointed as Lieutenant Governor of Jamaica, a function that allowed him to keep good sized effect within the Caribbean.

Later Life and Death:

Morgan's later years had been marked with the aid of political and social impact in Jamaica. He have become concerned in nearby politics, serving as appearing governor on numerous occasions. Despite his earlier piratical sports activities sports, Morgan died peacefully in 1688 in Jamaica, leaving in the back of a complex legacy that combined piracy, america of america-sanctioned plunder, and political electricity.

Legacy and Controversy:

Henry Morgan's legacy is one in every of contradictions and controversy. While celebrated in England as a hero and knight, he is remembered in Spanish-speaking regions as a ruthless pirate who terrorized their colonies. In present day instances, debates keep about whether or no longer to view Morgan as a cunning privateer, a rustic-backed pirate, or a ruthless crook.

Popular Culture:

Henry Morgan's existence has been romanticized and fictionalized in numerous styles of well-known way of life, along with literature, films, and tv. The individual of Captain Morgan, featured in diverse rum manufacturers, is loosely primarily based completely on the historical parent, similarly contributing to the iconic fascination collectively together with his story.

In quit, Henry Morgan's lifestyles represents a complex financial catastrophe within the statistics of piracy, privateering, and colonial expansion. His exploits inside the Caribbean, from a achievement raids to political maneuvering, make him a charming and arguable discern whose legacy keeps to captivate historians and fans alike.

Cheng I Sao

Cheng I Sao, additionally called Ching Shih or Zheng Yi Sao, became one of the handiest and a success pirates in information. Born in 1775 in Guangdong Province, China, Cheng I Sao rose from a humble historical past to come to be the chief of a massive pirate confederation, terrorizing the waters of the South China Sea finally of the early 19th century.

Early Life:

Cheng I Sao, at the start named Shi Yang, have grow to be a part of the Guangdong pirate community at a more youthful age. She married the notorious pirate Cheng I in 1801, stepping into a partnership that would later transform the maritime landscape inside the region.

Expansion of the Pirate Fleet:

After Cheng I's death in 1807, Cheng I Sao took command of the Red Flag Fleet, a formidable pirate armada that have been assembled with the aid of her overdue husband. With her strategic acumen and management capabilities, she stepped forward the fleet's gain and electricity, incorporating a diverse style of pirates, fishermen, and different maritime companies into her confederation.

Code of Laws:

One of Cheng I Sao's maximum superb achievements come to be the established order of a entire code of legal guidelines and guidelines to manipulate her pirate fleet. The code become a difficult and fast of suggestions and recommendations that dictated how the pirates were to conduct themselves, address disputes, and distribute loot. Breaking those guidelines often brought about excessive punishments, in conjunction with demise.

Fleet Structure and Organization:

Under Cheng I Sao's manipulate, the Red Flag Fleet grew to embody hundreds, if not masses, of ships and tens of loads of pirates. The fleet have become prepared into really one of a kind squadrons, every with its very non-public commander accountable for imposing Cheng I Sao's orders. This hierarchical form allowed for powerful coordination and manage over the giant pirate armada.

Pirate Operations:

Cheng I Sao's fleet operated significantly within the South China Sea, preying on issuer company vessels, fishing boats, or maybe military ships. Coastal villages and towns were pressured to pay safety cash to keep away from being pillaged via manner of the pirates. Cheng I Sao's control over the maritime exchange routes gave her extremely good impact in the area.

Negotiations with the Chinese Government:

As Cheng I Sao's strength and have an impact on grew, the Chinese government, led thru the Qing Dynasty, identified the want to cope with the pirate threat. In 1810, the Chinese government, below the command of naval officer Zhang Bao, initiated negotiations with Cheng I Sao. Remarkably, an settlement grow to be reached, permitting Cheng I Sao and her enthusiasts to retire peacefully with their loot in change for ceasing their piratical sports.

Later Life:

Following her retirement from piracy, Cheng I Sao and her husband's accompanied son, Cheung Po Tsai, lived a quite quiet lifestyles. Cheng I Sao controlled a gambling residence and operated a salt trade business agency, reportedly gathering giant wealth.

Legacy:

Cheng I Sao's legacy is one in every of exquisite control and strategic brilliance. Her functionality to unite numerous pirate factions, establish a useful code of criminal hints, and negotiate a non violent retirement with the Chinese government gadgets her apart as a completely unique decide in pirate data. The Red Flag Fleet's effect at the South China Sea persisted even after Cheng I Sao's retirement, influencing the region's maritime dynamics for years.

Representation in Popular Culture:

Cheng I Sao's tale has inspired severa works of literature, movie, and tv. Her existence and the exploits of the Red Flag Fleet were depicted in novels, documentaries, and films, showcasing the iconic fascination with this super woman who defied societal norms to emerge as one of the maximum a fulfillment pirates in records.

Chapter 10: Stede Bonnet

Stede Bonnet, often known as the "Gentleman Pirate," end up a infamous pirate inside the course of the "Golden Age of Piracy" inside the early 18th century. His tale is particular, as he defied the usual image of a pirate, being a rich and informed man who've end up to a lifestyles of piracy for motives that stay genuinely mysterious.

Early Life and Background:

Born spherical 1688 in Barbados, Stede Bonnet hailed from a wealthy plantation-owning family. He acquired an great schooling and, as a more youthful man, led a cushty lifestyles. However, however his privileged background, Bonnet's existence took an unexpected flip.

Turn to Piracy:

In 1717, Stede Bonnet's preference to end up a pirate bowled over his family and the local people. The specific reasons for his dramatic shift stay dubious. Some money owed endorse that he became affected by health problems and sought the seafaring lifestyles as a remedy, while others advocate that he may also moreover furthermore have been brought on by using the usage of dissatisfaction together along with his marriage or a choice for journey.

Outfitting the Revenge:

Bonnet used his exquisite wealth to outfit a deliver, which he named the Revenge. Despite his loss of maritime enjoy, he appointed an expert company to control the deliver, showcasing a diploma of naivety that might contribute to his later demanding situations as a pirate.

Pirate Career:

Bonnet's pirate career modified into marked with the aid of way of way of a sequence of successes and failures. Unlike many pirates of his time, he did no longer engage in violence unnecessarily, and he frequently desired to avoid warfare. However, this approach did no longer constantly sit down properly along together with his team, who may additionally have predicted a greater aggressive and worthwhile pirate captain.

Bonnet engaged in piracy alongside the Atlantic coast of the American colonies and the Caribbean, focused on service provider vessels and taking pictures prizes. He even sailed along the notorious Blackbeard for a quick length, forming an uneasy alliance.

Capture and Imprisonment:

Bonnet's career took a downturn whilst he emerge as captured with the useful useful resource of government in North Carolina in 1718. His institution scattered, and Bonnet changed into taken to Charleston, wherein he confronted trial for piracy. Despite his rich history, Bonnet turn out to be discovered accountable and sentenced to hold.

The Trial and Execution:

Stede Bonnet's trial in Charleston become super for its uncommon activities. Bonnet, representing himself at some point of the trial, pleaded responsible to all fees. His eloquence and obvious regret earned him some sympathy from the court and the overall public.

Despite his responsible plea, Bonnet turn out to be sentenced to loss of life, and he end up hanged in Charleston on December 10, 1718. His frame became left to recognize in chains as a caution to one-of-a-kind may need to-be pirates.

Legacy and Historical Perspective:

Stede Bonnet's tale is frequently visible as a weird anomaly in the annals of piracy because of his unexpected transition from a wealthy planter to a pirate captain. His as a substitute brief and tumultuous profession, marked thru each successes and failures, is a testomony to the complexities of pirate life in some unspecified time in the future of the Golden Age of Piracy.

In popular lifestyle, Stede Bonnet's story has been the problem of novels, performs, or even a character within the famous video game "Assassin's Creed IV: Black Flag." The "Gentleman Pirate" remains a fascinating ancient parent, illustrating the diverse motivations and backgrounds of folks that grew to emerge as to a existence of piracy in the course of this tumultuous length in maritime records.

Jean Lafitte

Jean Lafitte, a colourful and enigmatic determine of the early 19th century, played a substantial position in the international of piracy, privateering, and smuggling, particularly inside the Gulf of Mexico and the Caribbean in the course of the "Golden Age of Piracy."

Early Life:

Jean Lafitte's particular transport date is uncertain, however he changed into likely born in the early 1780s in both France or the

French colony of Saint-Domingue (modern-day-day Haiti). Lafitte and his elder brother, Pierre Lafitte, have become worried in privateering sports activities at a few level inside the Napoleonic Wars.

Move to Louisiana:

In the early 19th century, Jean Lafitte and his brother determined themselves in New Orleans, Louisiana. They established a smuggling operation and engaged in the illicit trade of goods, such as slaves and contraband. Lafitte fast have become a outstanding determine within the region, stated for his air of thriller and entrepreneurial spirit.

Barataria Bay:

The Lafitte brothers mounted a base in Barataria Bay, a community of waterways south of New Orleans. This location proved best for their smuggling and privateering sports, imparting smooth get proper of entry to to the Gulf of Mexico and its profitable trade routes.

Privateering and the War of 1812:

During the War of 1812, the USA authorities identified the ability charge of Lafitte's maritime understanding and issued privateering licenses to him and his pals. Lafitte's privateer fleet contributed extensively to the American reason, mainly during the Battle of New Orleans in 1815, in which they carried out a essential role in protecting the metropolis in competition to the British.

Conflict with the U.S. Government:

Despite Lafitte's assist sooner or later of the War of 1812, the U.S. Government have emerge as in opposition to him in the publish-conflict years. The government sought to suppress piracy and smuggling, and Lafitte's activities in Barataria Bay drew elevated scrutiny.

In 1817, the government issued a warrant for Lafitte's arrest, essential to a traumatic dating between him and the government. Lafitte, but, endured his operations, evading seize for a time.

The Battle of Barataria Bay:

In 1814 and 1817, the U.S. Navy completed raids on Lafitte's base in Barataria Bay, looking to dismantle his operation. Lafitte fought another time in what have emerge as known as the Battle of Barataria Bay. Despite Lafitte's resistance, the U.S. Navy in the long run succeeded in dispersing the pirate haven.

Galveston Island:

After the fall of Barataria Bay, Lafitte relocated to Galveston Island off the coast of Texas. There, he installation a modern day pirate haven and persevered his smuggling operations. Lafitte's have an effect on extended into the political opinions of the region, as he common alliances with privateers, pirates, and nearby Native American companies.

Later Years and Disappearance:

In the early 1820s, because the U.S. Government improved efforts to put off piracy, Lafitte faced mounting strain. In 1821, he not unusual an offer of a whole pardon from the Spanish government in change for ceasing his piracy sports sports. Lafitte and his enthusiasts abandoned Galveston, and Lafitte's subsequent activities live shrouded in mystery.

Legacy and Folklore:

Jean Lafitte's legacy is one in every of contradiction. While he engaged in criminal activities consisting of piracy and smuggling, he moreover carried out a vital function in defending New Orleans all through the War of 1812. Lafitte is remembered as a charismatic and foxy parent who navigated the complexities of the geopolitical panorama of his time.

In popular way of life, Jean Lafitte's story has been romanticized and fictionalized in numerous books, movies, and tv indicates. His complex person maintains to capture the creativeness, embodying the duality of the pirate as each a criminal and, in some instances, a hero protective closer to out of doors threats. The thriller surrounding Lafitte's later years and last future pleasant adds to the long-lasting appeal of this enigmatic discern in maritime statistics.

Samuel Bellamy

Samuel Bellamy, called "Black Sam," changed right into a infamous pirate throughout the "Golden Age of Piracy" inside the early 18th century. His brief but impactful profession, marked through audacious exploits and a sad give up, has left a long lasting legacy in the annals of pirate statistics.

Early Life and Career:

Born in 1689 in Devonshire, England, Samuel Bellamy to begin with led a traditional lifestyles, operating as a sailor and later as a ship's rigger. However, discontent together along with his existence and aspiring for wealth, he have turn out to be to piracy spherical 1715.

The Whydah Gally:

Bellamy's maximum famous deliver modified into the Whydah Gally, at first a slave deliver named the Whydah. Bellamy captured the vessel in 1717 off the coast of West Africa, changing it right into a powerful pirate supply. The Whydah became properly-armed and rapid, making it a great vessel for Bellamy's piratical interests.

Pirate Code:

Bellamy have become appeared for his democratic control style and adherence to a pirate code, a set of regulations governing his team's conduct and distribution of loot. His group had a say in desire-making, and Bellamy maintained a diploma of order and place on board, fostering a enjoy of organization spirit.

Audacious Raids:

Under Bellamy's command, the Whydah Gally have become a terror of the Atlantic. Bellamy focused a large type of ships, from small sloops to big merchant vessels. One of his most audacious captures come to be the Whydah's seizure of the Sultana, a carefully armed treasure deliver touring from the Caribbean to Europe.

Pirate's Republic:

Bellamy's fulfillment allowed him to set up a pirate's republic, a free confederation of pirates, on the Bahamas' island of New Providence. This length marked a short but intense duration of pirate self-governance within the area.

Downfall and the Storm:

In April 1717, the Whydah Gally met its tragic cease off the coast of Cape Cod. Caught in a violent nor'easter, the deliver sank, taking Bellamy and maximum of his team down with it. Only a few group individuals survived, and the Whydah's wreckage, along side its treasure, might stay undiscovered for loads of years.

Legacy and Rediscovery:

The Whydah Gally have emerge as a mythical shipwreck, often appeared as one of the most massive archaeological reveals in maritime statistics. In 1984, underwater explorer Barry Clifford determined the harm internet web web page off the coast of Cape Cod. The restoration efforts found an great array of artifacts, presenting treasured insights into the fabric manner of existence of pirates for the duration of the Golden Age.

Folklore and Popular Culture:

Samuel Bellamy's tale has grow to be part of pirate folklore and has been immortalized in severa books, documentaries, and movies. His romanticized picture as a democratic pirate captain and the tragic sinking of the Whydah Gally have captured the creativeness of humans global.

In summary, Samuel Bellamy's legacy lies in his formidable exploits, his adherence to a pirate code, and the tragic give up of the Whydah Gally. The discovery of the shipwreck centuries later has added a tangible measurement to the legend of Black Sam, contributing to ongoing fascination along together with his lifestyles and the Golden Age of Piracy.

Chapter 11: Charles Vane

Charles Vane, a notorious and ruthless pirate, accomplished a extraordinary feature at a few degree in the "Golden Age of Piracy" within the early 18th century. His bold exploits, violent inclinations, and confrontations with colonial government have left an indelible mark at the history of piracy.

Early Life and Beginnings:

Charles Vane's early life remains shrouded in thriller, with confined ancient data approximately his history. He probable started out his maritime profession as a sailor or privateer, undertaking valid and sanctioned acts of warfare at sea.

Turn to Piracy:

Vane's transformation right into a pirate happened round 1716 while he rejected the regulations of authority and embraced a existence of plunder. His charismatic management quick attracted a following, and he have grow to be one of the maximum feared figures within the Caribbean.

Pirate Raids and Tactics:

Charles Vane's modus operandi worried competitive and confrontational strategies. He changed into regarded for attacking ships with little regard for diplomatic niceties or the rules of engagement. Vane favored taking pictures vessels through stress, frequently taking satisfaction inside the chaos and violence that ensued during his raids.

Pirate Confederacy:

In 1718, Vane joined forces with other notorious pirates, together with Edward Teach (Blackbeard) and Benjamin Hornigold, to shape a unfastened confederation. This pirate alliance allowed them to coordinate their sports activities activities, percent records, and gift a united the the the front in competition to naval forces and colonial government.

Conflict with Governor Woodes Rogers:

Charles Vane's confrontations with authorities reached a climax sooner or later of the tenure of Governor Woodes Rogers in the Bahamas. Rogers, tasked with suppressing piracy, provided a desired pardon to pirates who surrendered voluntarily. Vane, however, adamantly refused any form of amnesty, rejecting the pardon and intensifying his attacks on British ships.

Escape and Continued Piracy:

Vane's refusal to absolutely take shipping of the pardon delivered approximately a dramatic showdown with naval forces in 1718. Rather than going thru certain seize, Vane escaped a British naval blockade with the resource of crusing his deliver immediately thru a narrow channel, narrowly heading off seize.

End of Piratical Career:

Vane's piratical profession met its result in 1719 at the same time as he encountered a French warship close to the Bahamas. Vane's organization, upset along along with his management and eager to genuinely take delivery of a French offer of clemency, mutinied closer to him. Vane became solid adrift in a small boat, leaving him marooned on a deserted island for a period.

Trial and Execution:

Charles Vane's properly fortune ultimately ran out even as he have become captured and taken to trial in Jamaica. Found accountable of piracy, Vane confronted the gallows. His final moments had been a defiant display of his refusal to put up to authority. Legend has it that, as he approached the gallows, Vane disdainfully kicked his executioner, maintaining that if he had to die, he would possibly die by using the palms of a gentleman.

Legacy and Historical Assessment:

Charles Vane's legacy is one in every of brutal and unrepentant piracy. His confrontational fashion, refusal to just accept a pardon, and very last loss of life on the gallows make a contribution to his image as a defiant and ruthless pirate captain. Vane's tale is frequently overshadowed via manner of contemporaries like Blackbeard, however his effect at the facts of piracy in the course of the Golden Age remains huge.

In famous way of life, Charles Vane's character has been depicted in various works, which includes the TV series "Black Sails," where he is portrayed as a foxy and ambitious pirate captain. While his life may additionally had been especially short-lived, Charles Vane's legacy endures as a part of the complex tapestry of the Golden Age of Piracy.

Grace O'Malley (Gráinne Mhaol)

Grace O'Malley, moreover called Gráinne Mhaol, turned into a mythical Irish pirate queen and chieftain who lived at a few stage in the sixteenth century. Her lifestyles is intertwined with the complicated records of Ireland, marked through political intrigue, maritime exploits, and a fierce spirit of independence.

Early Life and Background:

Grace O'Malley become born round 1530 into the Ó Máille dynasty, a seafaring family based in the western a part of Ireland. The O'Malleys were a outstanding extended family with a sturdy maritime life-style, and Grace grew up surrounded thru the rugged landscapes of County Mayo.

Early Maritime Ventures:

Grace's adolescence come to be marked with the beneficial resource of a deep connection to the sea. She reportedly decided her father on seafaring expeditions, gaining firsthand records of navigation, alternate, and naval method. As a young girl, she exhibited a eager interest in maritime affairs, an uncommon pursuit for a female in that generation.

Marriage and Widowed Leadership:

Grace O'Malley married Donal O'Flaherty, the chieftain of the O'Flaherty extended own family, in 1546. Their union bolstered the O'Malley have an effect on within the vicinity. However, Donal O'Flaherty modified into killed in an ambush, leaving Grace a widow with 3 children. Following her husband's demise, she lower again to her circle of relatives's maritime activities and took over manage of the O'Malley fleet.

Pirate Queen and Chieftaincy:

Embracing her feature as a leader, Grace O'Malley have turn out to be an impressive maritime determine. She commanded a fleet of ships and engaged in masses of sports sports, which embody alternate, fishing, and, in keeping with some bills, piracy. Her popularity as a expert sailor and tactician grew, incomes her the call of the "Pirate Queen."

Clashes with the English:

Grace O'Malley's sports activities delivered her into struggle with the English authorities, who sought to exert manage over Irish territories. The Tudor conquest of Ireland brought about progressed tensions, and Grace found herself at odds with Sir Richard Bingham, the governor of Connacht. Bingham centered Grace and her own family, main to a series of confrontations and reprisals.

Imprisonment and Political Maneuvering:

In 1593, Grace O'Malley became captured through the English on expenses of piracy. She have become imprisoned in Dublin Castle, but her incarceration was brief-lived. Grace's son, Tibbot Bourke, efficaciously lobbied for her launch. Grace then petitioned Queen Elizabeth I for restitution and the removal of Bingham, showcasing her political acumen and diplomatic talents.

Death and Legacy:

Grace O'Malley died around 1603, at a time whilst Ireland became gift technique large political and social modifications. Her death coincided with the surrender of the Tudor conquest, and her legacy endured as a photograph of Irish resistance and independence.

Folklore and Legends:

The lifestyles of Grace O'Malley is steeped in folklore and legends which have been exceeded down via generations. Tales of her fearlessness, negotiations with Queen Elizabeth I, and exploits at sea have emerge as an essential part of Irish mythology. The reminiscences of Gráinne Mhaol have been celebrated in conventional Irish ballads, poems, and modern literature.

Contemporary Influence:

In contemporary instances, Grace O'Malley remains celebrated as a symbol of Irish resilience and girl empowerment. Her legacy has stimulated innovative works, collectively with plays, novels, and musical compositions. Additionally, the revival of interest in her existence has added about efforts to discover and maintain internet web sites related to her, which incorporates her circle of relatives's citadel on Clare Island.

In end, Grace O'Malley's life is a testament to her resilience, management, and indomitable spirit inside the face of political and societal annoying situations. As the Pirate Queen of Ireland, she defied gender norms, commanded a fleet, and navigated the complex political landscape of her time, leaving a long lasting legacy as a picture of Irish identification and resistance.

Klaus Störtebeker

Klaus Störtebeker, a legendary determine from the "Golden Age of Piracy" within the past due 14th and early fifteenth centuries, turned into a German pirate who operated inside the waters of the North and Baltic Seas. His call has emerge as synonymous with the romanticized photograph of the pirate, and his exploits and eventual execution have been the hassle of severa memories, ballads, and legends.

Early Life:

Klaus Störtebeker's early life remains veiled in mystery, with few dependable historic records. It is concept that he became born in the past due 14th century, probably in Wismar, a port metropolis in Northern Germany. Some money owed suggest that he turned into a former privateer who turned to piracy, on the equal time as others advocate that he have turn out to be a pirate in reaction to economic and social upheavals of the time.

The Victual Brothers:

Störtebeker joined the Victual Brothers, a medieval privateer and pirate guild, at some point of a period of political turmoil known as the Hanseatic War. The Victual Brothers originated as mercenaries, stopping for the Hanseatic League, however they ultimately became to piracy. Störtebeker rose via the ranks and have become taken into consideration considered one of their maximum outstanding leaders.

Pirate Raids:

The Victual Brothers, under Störtebeker's leadership, engaged in piracy in the direction of company company vessels and Hanseatic League ships. They operated within the North and Baltic Seas, disrupting exchange routes and collecting massive wealth. Störtebeker's foxy techniques and audacious raids earned him each admiration and worry among sailors and coastal groups.

The Siege of Stockholm:

One of the most brilliant activities in Störtebeker's career come to be the Siege of Stockholm in 1395. The Victual Brothers, going through opposition from the Kalmar Union, laid siege to Stockholm. The metropolis ultimately capitulated, and Störtebeker and his men extracted sizable concessions and ransom.

Betrayal and Defeat:

Störtebeker's fortunes took a flip for the more intense whilst the alliance the various Victual Brothers and the Duke of Mecklenburg dissolved. In 1401, the Victual Brothers suffered a decisive defeat on the Battle of Hemmingstedt in opposition to the forces of the Hanseatic League. Störtebeker and his organization, going through overwhelming odds, retreated.

Capture and Trial:

In the aftermath of the Battle of Hemmingstedt, Störtebeker and a number of his organization had been captured with the aid of the Hanseatic League. They have been delivered to justice in Hamburg, wherein they faced a trial that modified into greater of a formality than a honest jail intending. Störtebeker modified into determined responsible of piracy and sentenced to dying.

The Execution:

On October 20, 1401, Klaus Störtebeker and his institution were finished in Hamburg. The approach of execution became beheading, however consistent with legend, the authorities furnished Störtebeker a deal: if he need to stroll beyond the headsman's block after being beheaded, he will be set free. In a very closing act of defiance, it is said that Störtebeker's headless body walked beyond a line of eleven of his guys in advance than collapsing.

Legacy and Legends:

The legend of Klaus Störtebeker has endured thru the centuries, with severa tales and ballads romanticizing his lifestyles and exploits. His call has grow to be synonymous with the archetype of the charismatic and ambitious pirate, resisting authority and preventing for a purpose.

Modern Representations:

Klaus Störtebeker's tale has inspired severa works of literature, theater, and film.

Numerous novels and historic debts have explored his lifestyles, each which include its very own embellishments to the already wealthy tapestry of legends surrounding him. Störtebeker's legacy is likewise celebrated in fairs and sports in Northern Germany, retaining the reminiscence of this medieval pirate alive in famous manner of life.

In precis, Klaus Störtebeker's life is a charming mixture of historical reality and mythical embellishment. His feature as a pirate chief for the duration of a tumultuous period in medieval Europe, mixed with the dramatic sports of his capture and execution, has secured his region in the pantheon of pirate lore. The enduring image of Störtebeker as a charismatic and fearless pirate captain continues to captivate the creativeness, making him a long-lasting photo of the romanticized era of piracy.

Chapter 12: William Fly

William Fly, a notorious English pirate, have become active eventually of the "Golden Age of Piracy" inside the early 18th century. His brief but impactful profession, marked with the useful resource of a series of violent encounters and a dramatic execution, offers a darkish financial disaster to the facts of piracy.

Early Life:

William Fly's early life is shrouded in obscurity, with little reliable facts approximately his heritage or upbringing. His journey into piracy isn't well-documented, however it is probable that monetary hardships or a seafaring historic past drew him to a life of crime at the high seas.

Pirate Career:

Fly's pirate career obtained notoriety inside the early 1720s even as he joined the crew of the supply Elizabeth, a vessel appeared for its brutal and lawless sports activities. Fly speedy rose via the ranks, ultimately becoming the supply's quartermaster—a characteristic that granted him huge authority a number of the organization.

The Elizabeth's Mutiny:

The crew of the Elizabeth, discontent with their brutal captain, Christopher Winter, staged a mutiny. They overthrew Winter and elected William Fly as their new captain. Under Fly's leadership, the supply continued its piratical sports, preying on vessels along the American coast.

The Capture of the Squirrel:

One of Fly's high-quality exploits changed into the seize of the Squirrel, a sloop commanded through Captain William Rhett. The team of the Squirrel, fearing a brutal future at the palms of Fly's pirates, surrendered without a combat. This victory boosted Fly's reputation among his organization and struck fear into the hearts of various sailors in the vicinity.

Dissent and Discord:

Despite his preliminary reputation a number of the group, Fly's management speedy faced demanding conditions. Some contributors of the institution grew dissatisfied together alongside with his command, especially as Fly tried to put into impact stricter subject. This discontent might finally purpose his downfall.

The Mutiny Against Fly:

In October 1726, on the identical time as anchored off the coast of Massachusetts, a dispute erupted amongst Fly and his group over the branch of spoils. Tensions escalated, and Fly's attempt to assert his authority led to a mutiny. The team, disappointed alongside along with his control, overpowered Fly and seized manipulate of the ship.

Capture, Trial, and Execution:

After the mutiny, Fly and numerous of his fans were captured and taken to Boston for trial. The trial changed into fast, and Fly faced costs of piracy. He completed his non-public protection however was placed responsible and sentenced to loss of lifestyles.

On July 12, 1726, William Fly have grow to be finished with the aid of setting in Boston. His frame changed into then gibbeted—displayed in a cage hung from a pole—as a caution to tremendous ought to-be pirates. This unpleasant shape of autopsy punishment aimed to discourage piracy thru using showcasing the excessive effects waiting for folks that engaged in such sports activities.

Legacy:

William Fly's legacy is one in every of violence, mutiny, and a gruesome quit. His quick however turbulent stint as a pirate captain, characterized with the aid of manner of the usage of inner strife and discord, stands as a cautionary tale within the broader narrative of piracy within the path of the Golden Age.

Historical Perspectives:

The ancient document surrounding William Fly is constrained, and lots of what is understood about him comes from trial data and cutting-edge-day payments. The ambiguity surrounding his early life and the brevity of his pirate profession make contributions to the mystique surrounding his call.

Cultural Depictions:

While not as widely romanticized or remembered as some other pirates of the generation, William Fly's tale has been explored in various historical debts and pirate-themed literature. His unsightly execution and the macabre show of his gibbeted frame had been mentioned in discussions approximately the harsh consequences meted out to pirates within the course of this era.

In cease, William Fly's existence and absence of existence encapsulate the brutality and threatening nature of piracy in the path of the Golden Age. His mutiny, seize, and grisly execution function a stark reminder of the dangers and consequences faced via individuals who determined on a lifestyles of crime on the immoderate seas in the early 18th century.

Thomas Tew

Thomas Tew, regularly known as Captain Kidd's predecessor inside the annals of pirate statistics, modified into an English privateer have become pirate who operated for the duration of the late seventeenth century, contributing to the infamous technology of the "Golden Age of Piracy." Tew's short but impactful career left an indelible mark on pirate lore.

Early Life and Privateering:

Thomas Tew become in all likelihood born in England inside the mid-seventeenth century, and little is notion approximately his childhood. He began his maritime career as a privateer, a central authority-sanctioned pirate employed to attack and plunder enemy ships in some unspecified time in the future of times of conflict. Privateering supplied a criminal framework for piracy, and Tew received treasured experience in naval struggle.

Turn to Piracy:

As the War of the Grand Alliance concluded within the late 17th century, many privateers discovered themselves unemployed. Tew, like numerous others, have become to piracy as a way of persevering with his useful and adventurous maritime sports activities. Around 1691, Tew joined the ranks of folks that rejected the restrictions of legality for the freedom and capacity wealth supplied by using way of piracy.

The Amity:

Tew secured a commission from the governor of Bermuda, Nathaniel Blakiston, allowing him to function as a privateer in competition to French and pirate vessels. However, Tew betrayed this take delivery of as actual with and instead used his deliver, the Amity, to embark on a pirate project within the Indian Ocean. The choice to expose pirate end up probable stimulated via the usage of the attraction of the East Indies, mentioned for its wealthy trade routes and precious cargo.

Indian Ocean Expedition:

Thomas Tew, in conjunction with one of a kind pirate captains, at the aspect of Henry Every, set sail for the Indian Ocean, focused at the beneficial change maximum of the East Indies and the Red Sea. The pirates sought to intercept and plunder the richly weighted down Mughal and East India Company vessels.

Capture of the Gunsway:

One of Tew's maximum massive exploits befell in September 1692 even as he and his group captured the Gunsway, a huge Mughal deliver carrying an splendid treasure. The plunder from this unmarried capture have come to be superb, and Tew's crew reportedly made off with massive wealth in gold, silver, and precious gem stones.

Death in Action:

Despite the success of his Indian Ocean tour, Thomas Tew's piratical career grow to be reduce short. In 1695, Tew engaged a heavily armed supply, the Fateh Muhammed, off the coast of Madagascar. During the war, Tew changed into struck thru a cannonball and killed, marking the surrender of his pirate career.

Legacy and Influence:

Thomas Tew's legacy is extraordinary for his ambitious task into the Indian Ocean and the extensive fulfillment he completed in a short span. The seize of the Gunsway made Tew and his institution immensely rich, but his loss of life left the future of his collected wealth uncertain.

Impact on Pirate Code:

Tew's day journey had broader implications for the pirate network. The massive wealth received raised tensions most of the institution participants, important to discussions about equitable distribution. This tension contributed to the established order of pirate codes, informal agreements among pirate crews outlining recommendations and processes for governance and wealth distribution.

The Fate of Tew's Treasure:

Following Tew's loss of existence, the destiny of his treasure have become a topic of speculation and intrigue. Some testimonies suggest that Tew's treasure have become divided among his group, at the identical time as others propose that it have become buried on an island. The elusive nature of Tew's wealth has fueled treasure-searching myths and legends.

Cultural Representations:

Thomas Tew's exploits have inspired numerous works of literature and movie, contributing to his enduring presence in well-known way of life. His adventures, along side the mystery surrounding the destiny of his treasure, preserve to capture the imagination of these interested by the Golden Age of Piracy.

In summary, Thomas Tew's profession as a pirate was marked through the use of audacity, fulfillment, and a tragic stop. His assignment into the Indian Ocean and the capture of the Gunsway underscored the wealth that is probably amassed via piracy. Tew's impact on the pirate network extended beyond his death, influencing the development of pirate codes and contributing to the enduring appeal of pirate lore within the pages of records.

Rahmah ibn Jabir al-Jalahimah

Rahmah ibn Jabir al-Jalahimah, also called Rahmah bin Jabir al-Jalahma, turn out to be a infamous Arab pirate who operated inside the

Persian Gulf inside the route of the early 19th century. His exploits and audacious sports have earned him an area in the annals of maritime records, and his tale is intertwined with the complicated political and economic dynamics of the area sooner or later of that point.

Early Life and Background:

Rahmah ibn Jabir al-Jalahimah became born in the overdue 18th century within the Arabian Peninsula. Little is thought about his adolescence, and records approximately his upbringing and training are scarce. It is believed that he got here from a Bedouin tribe, and his maritime profession emerged towards the backdrop of the flourishing change and political turbulence inside the Persian Gulf.

Rise to Piracy:

In the early 19th century, the Persian Gulf have become a hub of maritime change routes, connecting the Arabian Peninsula,

Iran, India, and beyond. Rahmah, pushed with the resource of a combination of financial motives and a desire for wealth and power, grew to turn out to be to piracy. The fragmented political landscape of the location, marked by the usage of the decline of traditional powers and the upward thrust of community rulers, supplied a conducive environment for piracy to flourish.

Pirate Confederacy:

Rahmah have become now not simply an character pirate but a key determine in a larger pirate confederacy that operated inside the Persian Gulf. This unfastened alliance of pirates, which include exclusive extremely good figures like Dawasir, Khadir bin Saif, and Jasim bin Jabir, sought to manipulate crucial maritime alternate routes, in particular the ones concerning beneficial cargoes which consist of pearls, spices, and special precious items.

Tactics and Targets:

Rahmah's pirate techniques have been characterized via fast and ambitious raids on ships navigating the waters of the Persian Gulf. His fleet of nicely-geared up dhows allowed him to technique unsuspecting vessels and overpower them brief. Rahmah's goals covered provider company ships, buying and selling vessels, or perhaps army ships, making him an impressive pressure inside the area.

Struggle Against European Powers:

As European powers sought to defend their alternate pursuits inside the Persian Gulf, conflicts with network pirates escalated. Rahmah and his confederacy engaged in confrontations with British and Portuguese naval forces. These clashes had been part of the wider European efforts to suppress piracy and set up manage over strategic waterways.

Capture and Imprisonment:

Rahmah's piratical sports activities drew the attention of colonial powers, especially the

British East India Company. In 1820, British naval forces, led via Captain James Loch, launched a marketing campaign to suppress piracy inside the Persian Gulf. Rahmah's stronghold at the island of Qeshm became a intention. After an extended naval engagement, Rahmah became captured and taken into British custody.

Trial and Execution:

Rahmah ibn Jabir al-Jalahimah confronted trial in Bombay (present-day Mumbai) in 1822. He became charged with piracy, homicide, and unique offenses. The trial ended in his conviction, and Rahmah modified into sentenced to death. In 1822, he changed into executed with the aid of putting, marking the save you of his infamous career as a pirate in the Persian Gulf.

Legacy and Historical Perspective:

Rahmah ibn Jabir al-Jalahimah's legacy is one in every of an impressive pirate who navigated the complex geopolitical panorama of the Persian Gulf within the route of a time of giant exchange. His exploits, along side the ones of his confederates, left an extended-lasting impact at the region's maritime statistics. Rahmah's tale is frequently invoked in discussions about the worrying conditions posed via manner of piracy and the efforts of colonial powers to preserve control over crucial alternate routes.

Cultural Representations:

Rahmah's existence has inspired severa cultural representations, which consist of novels, oldsters stories, and documentaries. His character is regularly depicted as a image of resistance toward foreign places dominance, embodying the complicated socio-political dynamics of the Persian Gulf in the 19th century.

In forestall, Rahmah ibn Jabir al-Jalahimah's life as a pirate inside the Persian Gulf gives a window into the tumultuous length of maritime records in the end of the early nineteenth century. His exploits, stressful situations in the direction of colonial powers, and eventual downfall contribute to the rich tapestry of pirate lore, making him a superb parent in the broader narrative of piracy in the Arabian seas.

Chapter 13: Bartolomeu Português

Bartolomeu Português emerges as a determine from the exciting era of buccaneering, characterised via maritime conflicts and privateering sports activities sports frequently in the Caribbean at a few stage within the 17th century. As a Portuguese buccaneer, he received notoriety for his attacks on Spanish delivery within the overdue 1660s, a time even as European powers have been often at odds within the New World.

Buccaneering in the seventeenth Century:

The seventeenth century changed into marked thru colonial rivalries and conflicts among European powers, particularly Spain, Portugal, England, and France, as they sought to set up dominance inside the profitable alternate routes of the Americas. Buccaneers had been essentially privateers, sanctioned via manner of European countries to assault enemy vessels and colonies inside the Caribbean.

Attacks on Spanish Shipping:

Bartolomeu Português, driven by way of a mixture of financial motives and the prevailing geopolitical tensions of the time, engaged in competitive actions within the route of Spanish delivery. The Caribbean, with its bustling trade routes and richly weighted down Spanish galleons, presented an appealing cause for buccaneers on the lookout for wealth and plunder.

Creation of the First "Pirate's Code":

One of Bartolomeu Português's maximum super contributions to pirate lore is attributed to the popularity quo of the primary "Pirate's Code." While the right contents and records of this code may not be nicely-documented, it's far believed to were a set of hints or guidelines governing the conduct and company of the buccaneer group.

The advent of a pirate code have become a realistic response to the stressful situations of pirate existence. It helped maintain order, area, and a degree of fairness a number of the group individuals. Such codes typically addressed problems much like the branch of loot, behavior inside the path of raids, and the decision of disputes.

Legacy of the Pirate's Code:

The concept of a pirate code have to evolve and grow to be more formalized inside the subsequent centuries at some point of the so-called "Golden Age of Piracy" in the past due 17th and early 18th centuries. Notable pirates like Bartholomew Roberts and Edward Teach (Blackbeard) might in all likelihood move directly to installation extra entire codes that meditated the democratic and egalitarian standards of pirate society.

Challenges and Demise:

Buccaneers like Bartolomeu Português confronted severa annoying situations inside the route of their careers. The steady hazard of naval retaliation, inner dissent amongst institution participants, and the perilous nature of pirate life made their endeavors precarious. The particular information of Português's lack of existence or the give up of his buccaneering career are not well-documented, leaving gaps within the historic narrative.

Impact on Pirate Lore:

Despite the constrained ancient facts, Bartolomeu Português's legacy endures via the concept of the early pirate code. The concept of a hard and rapid of policies governing pirate behavior have come to be a defining issue of pirate lore, influencing the romanticized image of pirates in literature, film, and famous lifestyle.

In precis, Bartolomeu Português, as a Portuguese buccaneer inside the overdue 17th century, contributed to the maritime conflicts of the time and is credited with the arrival of the number one pirate's code. His movements and the legacy of the code he installation have turn out to be a part of the broader narrative of piracy within the course of the buccaneering technology, shaping the perception of pirates for hundreds of years to go back.

François l'Olonnais

François l'Olonnais, a infamous French buccaneer and pirate lively at a few diploma within the mid-seventeenth century, stands out as one of the most ruthless and feared figures inside the information of piracy. His exploits, marked by way of the use of brutality and foxy strategies, have left an indelible mark on the technology called the "Golden Age of Piracy."

Early Life:

François l'Olonnais, born spherical 1635 in Les Sables-d'Olonne, France, commenced out his maritime profession as an indentured servant in the Caribbean. His early life became marred with the resource of servitude and hassle, however his strength of mind to get away this form of lifestyles fueled his adventure closer to a greater nefarious route.

Buccaneering inside the Caribbean:

During the mid-17th century, the Caribbean modified proper into a hotbed of buccaneering sports, a term that to start with mentioned French and English hunters who lived off the land by using manner of looking wild cattle and pigs. Over time, those hunters transitioned into piracy, preying on Spanish ships and settlements.

Rise to Infamy:

L'Olonnais rapid rose thru the ranks, gaining a fearsome recognition for his ruthless strategies and incessant pursuit of wealth. His group, crafted from fellow buccaneers, embraced his ferocity and foxy control style. L'Olonnais have become mentioned for his brutality, regularly torturing captives to extract facts about hidden treasures or to instill worry among ability adversaries.

Sack of Maracaibo:

One of L'Olonnais's maximum infamous exploits took place in 1667 whilst he led a daring raid on Maracaibo, a prosperous Spanish agreement in gift-day Venezuela. With a fleet of buccaneer ships, L'Olonnais navigated the tough terrain of the Zulia Lake and effectively sacked the metropolis. The raid delivered great wealth to the buccaneers, however it additionally solidified L'Olonnais's popularity as a merciless pirate.

Failed Attempt at Panama:

L'Olonnais, fueled via insatiable greed, set his factors of interest on Panama, a town rumored to be overflowing with riches. In 1668, he released into an unwell-fated day ride through the inhospitable jungles, going via harsh situations and fierce resistance from indigenous populations. The journey ended tragically for L'Olonnais as he became ambushed and killed through way of nearby warriors.

Legacy and Notoriety:

François l'Olonnais's legacy is considered one of brutality and infamy. His ruthless methods and cruel attacks on Spanish settlements earned him a place the diverse most feared pirates of his time. His tale have end up a cautionary story, illustrating the merciless realities of piracy and the precarious nature of a pirate's existence.

Cultural Representations:

L'Olonnais's life has inspired numerous literary works, which incorporates books and articles recounting his exploits. His individual has moreover made appearances in famous life-style, offering prominently in pirate-themed movies, documentaries, and video video video video games. The relentless and brutal nature of L'Olonnais's piracy has left an extended-lasting imprint at the romanticized photograph of pirates in entertainment.

Criticisms and Controversies:

While François l'Olonnais is remembered for his audacious exploits, his brutal techniques and the violence he inflicted on captives have also brought on grievance. Some historic money owed depict him as a psychopathic and sadistic determine, elevating ethical questions on the glorification of such ruthless individuals in pirate lore.

Historical Context:

Understanding L'Olonnais's moves calls for consideration of the ancient context. The Caribbean at some level inside the seventeenth century have emerge as a battleground for competing European powers, and piracy, usually, turned into a manner of resisting imperial dominance and seeking out personal wealth in a lawless surroundings.

In cease, François l'Olonnais's existence epitomizes the brutality and ambitious adventures of the buccaneers during the Golden Age of Piracy. His ruthless techniques, infamous raids, and tragic demise make contributions to the complex narrative of piracy inside the Caribbean, reflecting the merciless realities of a tumultuous era in maritime records.

Cheung Po Tsai

Cheung Po Tsai, a mythical decide in Chinese pirate records, become a infamous pirate energetic at a few level within the early 19th century. His tale is characterised via bold naval exploits, strategic brilliance, and a very unique aggregate of myth and truth that has captivated the imaginations of humans for generations.

Early Life and Background:

Cheung Po Tsai, whose call way "Cheung Po the Kid," changed into born in 1783 inside the Guangdong province of China. Originally named Cheung Po, he started out his lifestyles in a fishing village and later have become a pirate below the have an impact on of the notorious pirate Cheng I. Cheng I, stimulated thru Cheung Po's intelligence and courage, observed him as his son and groomed him for a control role in the pirate confederation.

Cheng I and the Pirate Confederation:

Cheng I, additionally called Zheng Yi or Cheng Yat, grow to be a powerful pirate who managed a huge pirate confederation inside the South China Sea. He united numerous pirate fleets below a common banner, growing a formidable stress that challenged every Chinese and overseas navies. Cheung Po Tsai rose to prominence within this confederation, demonstrating wonderful capabilities as a naval tactician and chief.

Leadership and Tactics:

After Cheng I's death in 1807, Cheung Po Tsai, collectively with Cheng's widow Cheng Shih, took control of the pirate fleet. Cheung Po Tsai's control abilties have grow to be evident as he expanded the pirate confederation's have an effect on, orchestrating raids and setting up dominance over coastal areas. His tactical brilliance and capability to navigate the complex waterways of the South China Sea made him an excellent adversary.

Infamy and Exploits:

Cheung Po Tsai's pirate fleet, such as masses of junks and thousands of pirates, terrorized the seas. They engaged in piracy, smuggling, and extortion, focused on carrier company vessels, coastal cities, and fishing agencies. Cheung Po Tsai's infamy grew, and his fleet have emerge as identified for its capability to elude naval government.

Surrender and Service:

In 1810, going thru extended stress from the Chinese and British navies, Cheung Po Tsai made the surprising choice to surrender. The terms of his give up had been negotiated, and Cheung Po Tsai and his pirates agreed to serve the Qing government in exchange for amnesty. This circulate allowed him to transition from a life of piracy to a position in the Chinese manipulate.

Later Life and Legacy:

Cheung Po Tsai's later lifestyles changed into marked via his carrier within the Qing army, wherein he completed a function in suppressing piracy. He became in the long run appointed as a naval officer, contributing his know-how of pirate techniques to combat piracy in the location. Some money owed endorse that he also can have even held a excessive-score characteristic inside the army.

Folklore and Cultural Impact:

Cheung Po Tsai's tale is deeply intertwined with Chinese folklore and famous way of existence. Numerous legends and myths surround his lifestyles, portraying him as a Robin Hood-like decide who stole from the rich and helped the poor. These tales had been retold in diverse forms, such as novels, operas, and movies, contributing to his enduring repute as a legendary pirate in Chinese statistics.

Historical Interpretations:

While Cheung Po Tsai's exploits are often romanticized in folklore, historic interpretations renowned the complexity of his individual. His give up and subsequent organization to the Qing authorities highlight the pragmatic selections made via pirates coping with developing stress from naval forces. The blending of historical fact and legend makes Cheung Po Tsai a captivating and enigmatic determine.

In quit, Cheung Po Tsai's existence is a charming mixture of ancient reality and delusion. His upward push as a pirate chief, strategic brilliance, surrender, and later company to the Qing government contribute to the multifaceted narrative of piracy within the South China Sea at some degree inside the early nineteenth century. Whether regarded as a fearsome pirate or a decide of folklore, Cheung Po Tsai stays a long lasting image of maritime journey and intrigue in Chinese information.

Chapter 14: Thomas White

Thomas White's maritime career commenced out in the Royal Navy, wherein he served as a sailor. His transition to the service provider trading vessel Marigold took him from Plymouth to Barbados, in which he assumed the location of captain. This length probable involved ordinary trade voyages, navigating the perilous waters recognized for every natural demanding situations and the looming threat of piracy.

Capture through way of French Pirates:

The turning factor in White's story happened off the coast of Guinea in 1698 on the same time because the Marigold fell prey to French pirates. In the chaotic stumble upon, the French pirates captured the Marigold and, tragically, killed some of English crewmen. However, White's fate took an surprising flip whilst a sympathetic French pirate spared his existence.

Refusal to Join Pirates and Enslavement:

Despite the mercy demonstrated thru the French pirate, White refused to join their ranks. In response, they subjected him to enslavement as an alternative. This choice now not to sign up for the pirates may additionally form the trajectory of White's subsequent research.

Escape and Adventures:

White seized an opportunity to get away captivity even as John Bowen and George Booth, likely acting as pirates, wrecked their supply near Madagascar in 1701. White's get away marked the start of a series of adventures wherein he determined himself aboard severa captured ships.

Joining Pirate William Read:

White's route intersected with the pirate William Read, and willingly, he joined Read's group. The existence of a pirate end up characterized through manner of a mix of camaraderie, lawlessness, and the pursuit of wealth through piracy. However, Read's lack of life at sea marked a shift in control, with Captain James assuming command.

Trading Vessels and Return to Port:

Under Captain James, the crew traded their vessel for a captured prize supply near Mayotte, an island within the Indian Ocean. This change typified the pirate workout of seizing and repurposing vessels for his or her very own dreams. The crew, under White's participation, went right now to capture numerous extra vessels earlier than ultimately returning to port.

Variations in Historical Accounts:

It's noteworthy that historic bills of White's reports may additionally moreover moreover range, reflecting the worrying situations of piecing together accurate narratives from fragmented and sometimes conflicting resources. Different versions of the tale exist, with variations in facts collectively with the instances of the French pirates' seize and the activities main to White's get away.

Themes in White's Narrative:

Thomas White's story encapsulates numerous habitual trouble matters in pirate lore in some unspecified time inside the future of the Golden Age. These encompass the capture and repurposing of vessels, the unpredictability of pirate life, and the complicated relationships among pirates. White's initial reluctance to enroll in the French pirates, his next break out, and his voluntary participation in piracy underneath specific leaders spotlight the fluid and dynamic nature of pirate allegiances.

Roche Braziliano

Roche Braziliano, a infamous parent in the annals of pirate history all through the Golden Age of Piracy, sticks out as one of the most colorful and enigmatic characters of his time. Born as Roch Brasiliano, he operated within the late seventeenth century, leaving in the back of a legacy that blends fact and legend, developing a charming narrative that has continued for masses of years.

Early Life and Origins:

Roche Braziliano's youth remains shrouded in thriller, adding an air of intrigue to his story. Believed to were born in Dutch Brazil (therefore his call), a former Dutch colony in South America, his real birthplace and date are uncertain. Little is understood approximately his upbringing or the sports that led him to a life of piracy.

Entry into Piracy:

Braziliano's adventure into piracy possibly started out out due to geopolitical shifts, conflicts, or private situations that drove human beings toward the lawless and profitable worldwide of piracy. The Caribbean and the Atlantic Ocean served due to the fact the backdrop for his piratical exploits, a place teeming with maritime exchange and possibilities for plunder.

Pirate Allies and Rivals:

Braziliano operated all through a time while pirate crews regularly fashioned loose alliances and rivalries. He sailed along notorious pirates, collectively with Captain John Davis, and characteristic grow to be related to exclusive famous figures like Captain George Booth. These alliances achieved a essential feature in the dynamics of pirate sports inside the West Indies and the Atlantic.

Notable Exploits and Raids:

Roche Braziliano's name have turn out to be synonymous with bold raids and audacious exploits. Like many pirates of his time, he focused Spanish and Portuguese vessels, encumbered with riches from the New World. Braziliano's raids were characterised with the resource of manner of brutality, and he have turn out to be identified to be a ruthless adversary, displaying little mercy to folks that crossed his route.

Brazilian Slave Revolt:

One infamous episode related to Roche Braziliano is his involvement in a Brazilian slave riot. Allegedly, Braziliano led a band of pirates in guide of a slave insurrection closer to Dutch authorities in Recife, Brazil. This event, if actual, affords a layer of complexity to Braziliano's character, depicting him now not handiest as a pirate but also as a player in broader social and political upheavals.

Capture and Escape:

Braziliano's piracy profession have become marked by the usage of every triumphs and setbacks. At one element, he confronted capture and imprisonment. However, he controlled a formidable get away, showcasing his resourcefulness and capability to navigate the traumatic conditions of captivity.

The Pirate Republic of Libertatia:

Roche Braziliano is sometimes related to the mythical pirate utopia called Libertatia. According to 3 money owed, he modified into some of the pirates who supposedly hooked up a democratic and egalitarian society on the island of Madagascar. However, the historic veracity of Libertatia stays a topic of discussion amongst historians.

Disappearance and Mystery:

The latter a part of Roche Braziliano's lifestyles is shrouded in thriller. Some debts recommend that he disappeared with out a touch, including an element of intrigue to his story. The lack of definitive information approximately his future has fueled hypothesis and contributed to the long-lasting mystique surrounding this pirate captain.

Legacy and Cultural Impact:

Roche Braziliano's legacy extends past the ancient report, as his exploits had been immortalized in literature, folklore, and famous way of life. His person has made appearances in diverse pirate-themed works, contributing to the romanticized picture of piracy in books, movies, and exclusive styles of leisure.

www.ingramcontent.com/pod-product-compliance
Lightning Source LLC
Chambersburg PA
CBHW070734020526
44118CB00035B/1345